# AWAKENING
## YOUR INNER LIGHT

This book is dedicated to
my two children, *Jason* and *Christal*,
to the healing of the earth and all her peoples,
and to the cessation of all suffering in the universe.

*One of the greatest gifts of Spirit is Life*
*Live to Be fully Human*
*To live within your Human-ity*
*Without Self-judgment or Denial*
*Is the most spiritual experience on Earth.*

*This book is dedicated to living this reality in our daily life.*

*. . . Aeoliah*

christmas 1993.

Dear, dear Andrew.

Beyond any problems we may have,
we have a very special love.
both of us won't find another one
It hasn't been easy for us lately:
it seems that there's always
something holding us apart.
It's not a question of who is to blame,
because we're both being ourselves,
and there's no fault in that.
Beneath it all,
We have something worthwhile,
and if we can sort through the
confusion,
we can find the happiness
we both want.
I think our love is worth it.

I know you're worth it

I love you
Zwaan.

# AWAKENING
## YOUR INNER LIGHT

*Healing Self-Abuse and*
*Reclaiming Your True Identity*

**Aeoliah Kuthumy**

A

HELIOS
RISING
PUBLICATION

HELIOS PUBLICATIONS
PO Box 151439
San Rafael, CA 94915

All inquiries should be addressed to HELIOS PUBLICATIONS.


LIBRARY OF CONGRESS CATALOGING IN PUBLICATION DATA

Kuthumy, Aeoliah.
    Awakening your inner light.

        Bibliography:
    1.  Self-Help, Psychology
    2.  Human Development, Spirituality

92-72541
ISBN 0-9633249-3-4

Cover: *Angel of Healing* by Aeoliah

Printed and bound in the United States of America

# TABLE OF CONTENTS

i

iii

## ACKNOWLEDGMENTS

I want to thank my *mother* and *father* for giving me birth, and for all their love and support. I would also like to acknowledge *Cheryll Melott* for all her assistance with typesetting, format and editing, and all of the following friends and people who have encouraged and supported me in making this publication a reality: *Jenna Eichten, Liv Ullman, Elisa Rapior, Ixthara Atlan, David and Linda MacKay, Carmen Balhestero, Erik Berglund, Carol Gentle, Cheryle Winn, Doni and Sadha Smith, Helche Köppen-Weber, Olivia Seijo, Aeona, Norman Miller, Iasos, Ken Jenkins, Robert Rose, Desiree Khan,* and all my other friends and associates. I also wish to acknowledge and thank all the loving, interdimensional *Light Beings* and *Ascended Masters* who have poured their precious love-vibrations and divine intelligence through me into this book.

I also wish to thank all my readers, and all of you wonderful beings around the world who have been "tuning in" to my music for the past twelve years. Thank you for all your love and support. You have all contributed greatly to the physical manifestation of this new creation.

*May the love, light and wisdom of this book guide you into your total healing, illumination and freedom.*

Love,

*Aeoliah Kuthumy*

Aeoliah Kuthumy

# PREFACE

Dear Reader:

This book was created to assist you in your journey of spiritual awakening, personal transformation, and healing. The major human issues of healing during the present time of our planetary and personal awakening relate to three basic primary aspects of our human development. These are:

1. Issues of **survival**, and how we relate to the **physical plane.**
2. Our evolving human **sexuality.**
3. Our **emotional development and emotional needs.**

As these three areas of human development are now in such major transition, transformation, and healing, it has become increasingly important in my own life to find practical and effective forms of transformation and healing that are able to penetrate deep into the inner core and cause of our human suffering and self-imposed limitations.

During the process of writing this book, I received many levels of self-healing and major shifts in my own conscious awareness have guided me into a more fulfilling life of wholeness, joy, and freedom. There were also times when I would swim in my own tears, cradling my wounded inner child, and listening intently to its cries or suppressed grief. Then there would be soft rainbows after raging storms and the calm serene peace that follows a major release. It takes just a little bit of love, care, and some courage to penetrate into those deep vulnerable places, and set them free. It also takes the commitment to care for one's own life that gives us the initiative to take this first step toward our own personal transformation and healing. As the book was progressing, I began writing to my inner child, and after a while realized that I was also writing to the inner child of every person on this earth. This awareness opened my heart to an even greater and deeper level of love and compassion for life and humanity. It was out of this growing love and union with all of life from which the vision and purpose of this book was born. At the same time, I was also healing my relationship between myself and the outer world.

This inner awakening took form through some of the chapters in this book. The process of creative synthesis and introspection, facilitated a major healing and transformation between my inner self and its relationship to outer reality. Old belief systems, spiritual concepts, and limiting perception patterns began to dissolve in order to make room for this new birth. My gift is to share my personal, transpersonal, and universal transformation with you, your inner child, and the Master within you. As you read the pages of this book, know that our love is merging and co-creating new dimensions of clarity, purpose, nurturing self-acceptance, and release, as we heal the illusion of duality and the cause and effect of all self-abuse.

May your journey be filled with Light and Love as you ascend into your True Identity and Freedom.

Love,

Aeoliah

# INTRODUCTION

We spend a whole lifetime changing and readjusting our perceptions in order to experience life more fully. Yet behind those perceptions are worlds within us that remain unexplored, waiting to be rediscovered, as we search for the hidden meaning of Life.

Life is a journey through the valleys, mountains, and oceans of consciousness. It is much like learning how to ski, to jump, to fall, to swim, to fly, and to walk. How do we transcend self-imposed limitations? How do we learn not to project our own vision of reality onto others? How do we learn to acknowledge and honor our own vision of reality without seeking approval and acceptance from others? How do we cope with the surfacing conflicts between our magnetic sexual desires and our spiritual awakening? How do we integrate the two? What is the meaning of true power and how can we learn the balanced use of this power for the benefit of all life and ourselves? How do we cope with, relate to, and heal the conflicts of duality, separation and polarity within our own individual consciousness and perceptions?

We as human beings face all of these major issues of human growth on the living stage of our daily life. How we respond and deal with these issues determines our present reality and personal human evolution on earth. If we simply wish to stay focused on only the "positives", we will continue to manifest situations and experiences in which the opposite polarity will inevitably surface and manifest itself. This is especially true if we are not in touch with our human emotions. Because all of us have

vii

experienced pain, rejection and some form of abandonment, there are deep-seated programs within our subconscious mind that act out these negative polarities over
and over again until they are faced, acknowledged, healed,
and released. Somewhere along life's path, (for most of us
this happens in childhood, during birth, or during a
previous incarnation) we accepted these experiences as
the only reality we were capable of living at the time. Our
inner child did not know how to shield itself from energies or projections of anger, resentment, lack, fear, and
the general insecurity that underlies most husband/wife
relationships. We had no other role models. We learned
from our parents and the world around us what is *good
and bad* or *right and wrong*, and we assimilated like
sponges absorbing energy and information in a purely
automatic, intuitive, spontaneous, non-discriminating
way. Tremendous invalidations from the unconscious
projections of both parents and society created a natural
defense mechanism within our inner child that was trig-
gered every time these feelings or emotions surfaced in
daily reality. Whether from parents, uncles, sisters, other
adults, or other children in the world, the trigger was
pulled in many different directions manifesting itself in
feelings of unworthiness, mistrust, and a general helplessness in coping with uncontrollable emotions. These
experiences became such a source of frustration for the
child that a pattern and series of defense mechanisms set
in to protect itself from further intrusion, projections,
hurt, pain and attacks. Remember, as children, we have
no frame of reference except the role model of our parents, or whoever is raising us at the time.

It is the purpose of the Part I and II of this book to
become aware of any unhealed issues of our own "inner

child" and to learn to re-awaken the trust and security that was denied us or lost during the critical years of our early development.

At the present stage of our planetary and human development the first three energy centers (or chakras) of the physical body need the most attention, understanding, acceptance, healing. and transformation. One of the major challenges is acknowledging and 'getting in touch with' our self-denial, self-doubt, self-judgment, guilt, shame and other major issues of abuse that started during early childhood. The main focus of the first few chapters of this book deal with the understanding, illumination, and healing of the three primary energy centers (chakras) and aspects of our human development:

1. **Base of Spine Center** .... **Survival**
   How we relate to the physical plane, our physical body, etc.
2. **Sacrum Center** .... **Our Sexual Development** and identity.
3. **Solar Plexus Center** .... **Our Emotional Development** and emotional needs.

If any of these three energy centers (chakras) are blocked, we will experience various forms of dysfunctional behavior such as resistance, obstruction, fear, scarcity, emotional inhibition, feelings of unworthiness, sexual abuse, and other forms of abuse.

We first look at the cause of self-abuse, what started the abuse, and what we can do to heal these recurring patterns of dysfunctional behavior. We begin our healing by clearing these first three energy centers. This is the place where we encounter the most resistance, judgments, addictions, suppression, denial and fears. We encounter human issues such as the fear of intimacy, trust, surrender, physical survival, emotional and sexual needs, learning to express our feelings and really being in touch with how we feel without losing our personal power or identity. Before we can effectively clear any of these blockages of energy, we must first get in touch with the **cause** that created this dysfunctional pattern of abuse, and how our subconscious mind interacts in this obstruction process. As we begin to understand our need for love, we begin to embrace all the primal human needs and urges of our first three centers, such as our sexual desires, emotional needs and our human vulnerabilities as an integral part of our human development and spiritual awakening. This is the first step toward healing the illusion of duality.

As you progress further into the book, we move into the higher energy centers of the heart, throat, third eye and crown. As we clear the cause and effect of our self-denial and self-abuse, we are ready to reclaim our true power, identity, and freedom.

# Introductory Chapter

# THE FOUR BODIES OF HUMAN ENERGY

There are four major centers of conscious energy and activity that comprise human development. I will from time to time refer to these four basic bodies throughout the book. They are as follows:

### THE ETHERIC BODY

This is an area within and around your body that is a living record of all past actions, experiences, and impressions both in and out of physical embodiment, and inbetween incarnations on other dimensions. It is a blueprint of our soul's evolution. Your etheric body corresponds to the energy field in your aura. All your life's experiences, the thoughts you think, the feelings you feel, all have a corresponding effect within the eight energy centers of the body (chakras). The vibratory rate of these centers are reflected in an energy field around your physical body known as the AURA. (See Color Plate 2) Within this aura are light and color frequencies that are ever changing depending on the state of your mental, emotional, and physical being. Since all the memories and causes of all life experiences are stored here, it is wise, therefore, to begin any healing process by first clearing the etheric body. It contains all the **causal**, (and collective) impressions and experiences ever known to your soul. This includes sub-conscious as well as conscious activities of the past and present.

## THE MENTAL BODY

This is an area of our being where thoughts and ideas are born. According to the development of our etheric body, our mental body (being a direct extension of our past experiences) is very much influenced by the impressions, memories and experiences stored within the etheric body. There is naturally great power within the mind to heal, transform and re-write old, dysfunctional life scripts. A purification and clearing of the etheric body and the impressions and great influence it has upon the mind must first take place. Learning how to empty the mind of pre-conceived concepts and limiting belief patterns opens up a new space within our mental body to create new and effective programs that are healing and beneficial to our emotional, physical and spiritual development. Naturally the process of discernment is a major tool in developing greater awareness and clarity of purpose when working with the mental body.

It takes great awareness, care and self-discipline not to allow the mind to simply become a repetitive, reactive pattern that unconsciously and blindly plays out the effect of our past actions (etheric body). To heal and transform our mental activity takes commitment and steadiness of purpose in order to dissolve and restructure old thought patterns that are no longer of service. It is a time of making vital choices in order to accelerate our healing and evolutionary process from the unconscious, reactive, 'victim' role pattern played out 'on a treadmill' to the victory of conscious co-creation, self-mastery, and freedom.

## EMOTIONAL BODY

Needless to say, this is the most challenging and un-healed area of human evolution. The emotional body has such a dramatic impact on our relationships and expressions of love. Once again, the filtering process from the mental body has a direct and profound effect on our emotional well-being. The cause initially begins in the etheric body, then is transferred through conscious awareness into the mental body. Then the mental body sends its signals and impressions to our brain and throughout the entire nervous system as we begin to experience feelings, impressions and reactions within our emotional body. The emotional energy center is located within our abdomen region, known as the solar plexus. Depending on the development and purity of our mind, our emotional body can be a tiring and repetitive roller coaster ride that 'plays out' its dramas from the treadmill of a mind that is still imprisoned by energies that have not been cleared in the etheric body. **You can clearly see the chain reaction from one state to another, if the initial clearing does not take place first in the causal (etheric body) area of our being.** If the mind becomes more disciplined and aware, the emotional responses will in turn become more refined and less reactive. On the other hand, if one is too much in the mind, not acknowledging true feelings, the emotional body suffers and becomes greatly imbalanced, causing a major blockage in the flow of energy in our solar plexus. This affects the flow of our life essence and sexual energy as it cannot easily flow upwards from the base of our spine into the crown center if there is any obstruction in any energy center. When our emotional body is blocked, it paralyses our ability to feel and express our emotions, which in turn makes it impossible for us to surrender to pure, unconditional love.

It takes great courage to allow our inner child to express its free and unsuppressed emotions and feelings without any self-judgment, guilt or shame. I deeply encourage all my clients to allow themselves to feel and experience any unhealed emotions of the inner child, so they can connect with whatever emotions or feelings were denied expression during childhood. During the vital process of introspection by looking into any feelings that were not allowed to express themselves freely during childhood, we begin to re-parent our inner child by giving it greater love, nurturing and self-acceptance. This opens the door to a healthier, more open expression of love, as we heal all the de-sensitized feelings that were suppressed during our early childhood. As we allow ourselves to experience and express more openly any emotions that need healing, we are gradually creating a stable foundation and environment for a new, re-established Trust in which our inner child can be nurtured, loved, and accepted.

## THE PHYSICAL BODY

The physical body is a remarkable living instrument created to help us evolve into more loving, conscious beings. Our physical body responds directly to any vibration or stimulus that it receives. If you nurture it with love and healthy, life-supporting thoughts and actions, you will have a body that will serve you in radiant health, vitality, and energy. Just as important as eating pure, whole and unprocessed foods, it is equally important to have "pure food for thought". As the mind and emotions greatly affect our physical health, one can see the importance and value of keeping a vital balance between our mind, physical body, and our emotional, feeling world.

Often when experiences from the distant past (other lifetimes and past experiences) are not healed within the etheric body, we will have a more difficult time coping with our mental and emotional states. This condition is especially amplified during our present cycle of planetary evolution, as the new frequencies and 'stepped-up' vibrations are accelerating the need for the clearing and healing of the etheric body. Any emotional issues that have been ignored and left unhealed from the past will surface more quickly now, so that we can release them and move on to greater wholeness in the present.

In the case when the mental and emotional bodies are not cleared, our physical well-being on one level or another will be directly affected. This may appear in the form of experiencing stress, nervous tension, sexual repression or abuse, or biochemical imbalances in our physical body. There are atoms and electrons within our physical body that transmit thought vibrations from our mind and feeling worlds (cell memory). There is an intelligence within these cells that carries the impressions from our etheric body through the electrons that circle around the atomic structure of our physical body. Once again, we can see the importance of treating the physical body with great respect as an active, living intelligence that responds immediately to all the input and stimulus it receives directly from us and from the world around us.

This is another reason why positive, healing affirmations are so powerful and effective in helping to clear limiting programs that the physical cells of the body have absorbed. Some cells are literally contracting and suffocating from the abuse that we subconsciously inflict upon them. Remember that the key to radiant health is a free flow of energy between all of these four bodies, the etheric, the mental, the emotional and the physical. When all four of these are in harmony with one another, there is a state of equilibrium, vitality, clarity and well-being within and without.

## THE VITAL BALANCING, REINTEGRATION AND HEALING OF THE FOUR BODIES

The following exercise is a very simple yet powerful tool in clearing and re-balancing the four bodies. I highly recommend doing this exercise at least twice daily, especially in the morning before you start your day, and just before going to bed. You will notice major adjustments in your energy field as well as in your physical body when you start to practice this meditation regularly. The exercise focuses on conscious breathing patterns combined with verbal affirmations.

If you like, you can make a personalized recording of the following affirmations for each of the four bodies with your own voice. This recording can be enhanced with soft healing music in the background. When you begin your breathing exercise, you may start the cassette and just focus on rhythmic breathing. This exercise will also expand your capacity for breathing slower and more deeply. The more you practice it, the easier it gets, until it becomes almost automatic.

1. As you **inbreathe**, inhale slowly and evenly, silently affirming to yourself (or listening to your own voice affirmation tape): "I AM **INBREATHING** GOD'S LOVE AND HEALING INTO MY ETHERIC BODY." Visualize white-golden Light enfolding your whole body until it fills your aura. This clears the etheric body. After you fully inhale, hold your breath and move to step two.

2. As you **hold your breath**, affirm silently: "I AM **ABSORBING** GOD'S LOVE AND HEALING INTO MY

MENTAL BODY." Visualize your entire head and crown absorbing white-golden Light. This is clearing your mental body.

3. As you begin **exhaling** (do this slowly and gradually), affirm: "I AM **EXPANDING** GOD'S LOVE AND HEALING INTO MY EMOTIONAL BODY." Visualize white-golden Light pouring into your solar plexus, clearing your emotions.

4. **After exhaling, hold your breath,** and affirm: "I AM **PROJECTING** GOD'S LOVE AND HEALING INTO EVERY CELL, ATOM, TISSUE AND ORGAN OF MY PHYSICAL BODY." Visualize white-golden Light entering your body permeating every cell and atom.

Repeat the above process, numbers 1 through 4, in succession of at least ten to twelve times in the morning and before sleep. As you begin repeating this breathing and affirmation exercise, you will notice that with regular practice, your breathing capacity will be much greater, longer and slower. I recommend starting each of the four breathing steps for a count of five seconds. In a few days you will be able to progress to seven seconds, and eventually to ten and twelve seconds. This entire breathing exercise is very beneficial to your health and highly reduces stress and tension in the body. If you choose to make a recording of your own voice for the affirmations, do so with great feeling, reverence and respect for your God Presence, as all the loving energy and awareness that you input will immediately be reflected in your outer world experiences.

EMBRACING THE HUMAN JOURNEY

Patience on Earth
Is a discipline;
To pass through the illusions of time and
Dancing through all the comings and goings daily
Without resistance
Is the strength and achievement
of a Master;
Not to get flustered when obstacles arise,
Using it as an opportunity to shift our gears and
Expand the flexibility of our creative
Self-Awareness
Obstacles, challenges that we create for ourselves
Until the cause is healed
Through the loving acceptance of
Our own human creation;
I dance the dance and
Then I move on to a finer Tune, and
One even subtler, but filled with more Light,
Beckons me deeper into the Essence of my Being
When I learn to embrace the density of each moment,
Each dance as it unfolds layers and layers of
Awakening Love and Remembrance
PATIENCE WITH YOURSELF
Is a discipline that passes through all the
Illusions of time, space, and all duality.

# PART I

# HEALING OUR PHYSICAL
# AND SEXUAL IDENTITY

FROM WITHIN THE HEART OF GOD

LIGHT IS BORN.

FROM THAT LIGHT

A FLOWER BLOOMS.


WITHIN THE HEART OF MAN

IS A FLAME

THAT HOLDS THE SEED

OF THE ENTIRE UNIVERSE.

# 1

# SURVIVAL:
# ACCEPTING OUR PHYSICAL IDENTITY

The primal instinct to live and to survive is one of the most basic drives and desires of all creatures. Unfortunately it is not just animals that will kill for their survival but humans as well. Great fear overshadows this primal instinct, especially in this threatening time of economic degeneration and political instability within human society. How to create new systems of life support without having to depend upon the dysfunctional and decaying socio-economic institutions has become an important issue to many people. If we experience lack in our life, we usually blame it on an external source, system or power. The first step in reclaiming your own power for personal survival is to recognize that any lack you are experiencing is the direct result of a limiting belief system, thoughts and feelings that are no longer serving to fulfill your basic needs for physical survival. This 'lack' within our personal identity is something that each one of us must be willing to see and recognize, so we can fill the inert space with love, light and healing. This nurturing process will gradually transform our limiting beliefs, thoughts and feelings into useful, fulfilling thoughts and actions that will reflect a new level of self love and healing as we then begin to take full responsibility for our lives.

The first step is to take full responsibility for our own fear or any experience of lack. We always think that it's money, or parents, or partner that's the problem. However, it is not so simple. Usually there is a mental or emotional block that sabotages any belief that we can really have whatever we may need or want in life. The second step is to fully ACCEPT OUR PHYSICAL INCARNATION as the creation of our own personal choice that we made to assist us in our spiritual awakening. Any resistance and discontent with this "chosen" life situation is what stops most of us from going any further. We really don't feel like being here. If we are sending out feelings that we don't want to be here, the universe cannot supply us with what we need. Any judgment we have about the "insane asylum" we created here on earth will be reflected in our personal interaction with others. Basically the entire planet is in a state of collapsing and major dysfunction, and has been for a long time! The "only way out is to go within" by creating stable patterns of support and inner healing that will bring true, lasting joy and fulfillment into your life on earth.

One of the major keys to receiving what you want in life is to begin SHARING more with others what you already have. This doesn't always have to be something material, but could be in the form of giving someone a massage, going for a walk with them, or just listening to someone's feelings with an open heart. It could be cooking a meal for someone, treating someone to dinner or lunch without expecting anything in return. Anything that is given selflessly out of love without expectation of a return usually comes back tenfold to the giver. This is the law of life – the more you share and give of yourself, the more is given to you as a glad free gift of the universe.

Even if you don't think you have much to offer, share the little that you do have and you will experience more abundance returning to you. **Sharing is trusting and knowing that the true and real abundance comes from the heart.** This is another key in healing major issues of survival. As you expand your capacity to serve others by sharing a part of yourself, whatever it may be, you are opening the doors of greater prosperity to come into your life.

Caring for your physical body is another tool that magnetizes greater support from the universe. The kind of foods you eat, how you care for your physical body "temple", the colors you wear, the kind of energy that you choose to have around you, all of this contributes to greater health and acceptance of the physical part of yourself. Learning great respect for the amazing function of your organs, cells, and all the millions of tiny openings in your skin also embraces the life support of your physical body. Being more in touch with your physical body through yoga or physical exercise also helps to stabilize and ground your energy into the physical plane, making your presence on the planet easier and more enjoyable. How you feel about your physical body also determines what you create in your external environment. Learning to love and accept all parts of your body is a very important key issue for creating abundance. Practice by thanking your physical body for the incredible, life-supporting service it is giving you and humanity. Just try this for about a month! Take a few moments each day, center yourself, and just get in touch with all parts of your body. Thank your body elemental and all the life force within your cells, tissues and organs; thank them for their service in maintaining and supporting the life within you. Becoming more conscious and grateful for the service of your physical body expands your own capacity for greater radiant health and abundance. Expressing sincere gratitude opens the inner chambers of the heart.

Start to visualize the abundance of the earth opening her arms to you, giving you everything you need in life. Learn to give something back to life as you share a special gift with others and the earth. Yours is a special gift to share with others on the earth. Plant a tree, make a garden, or share an apple with someone. As we raise the quality of vibration of our own life by healing our emotions, feelings and thoughts, we will shift from the primal mode of basic survival and existence into a higher and more meaningful LIFE of joy and fulfillment. By being kind to all of life around you and honoring and caring for the life within your SELF, you will raise the quality of your own LIFE, AS WELL AS EXPAND THE LIFE SUPPORT SYSTEM OF THE ENTIRE PLANET EARTH.

# 2

# HEALING AND ACCEPTING
# OUR SEXUALITY

As humans, we have not really awakened to the full potential and healing power that our sexuality can provide. As our patterns of self-abuse and control begin to dissolve and we initiate the healing of our emotional body, our sexuality begins to reflect a new level of wholeness, pleasure and ease that allows the fiery energy of this vital center to flow more freely throughout the rest of our body. Sexuality is a necessary and basic part of human life, like eating, sleeping and breathing. As humans, we are sexual beings with active human desires and needs. To suppress or deny this part of yourself actually diminishes the vitality of your very own creative life force.

During the present state of our human development, very few of us have healed the emotional body to the point where we are completely free and liberated in our sexual expression and identity. Because human society has created so many false role models, images and formulas for "being sexy", a tremendous overemphasis on "performing" has resulted in great dysfunctional patterns of abuse. This very act of pressure to "perform" and "please" has become one of the greatest stumbling blocks to the healing and fulfillment of our psycho-sexual natures. It desensitizes the natural flow of spontaneity and intuitive exploration of intimacy between two people. The tremendous abuse of personal power and greed to control others through the manipulation of this vital energy center throughout the centuries has also contributed to the corruption and dysfunction of this pure creative life force essence. The fear that this abuse has created in personal relationships within the mass consciousness of humanity is staggering.

Many lightworkers who have had previous incarnations in spiritual centers of learning such as monasteries, ashrams, and religious temples were taught that sexuality is not spiritual and is something that must be transcended or avoided. Many of these older teachings still prevail. This indoctrination, received and accepted through many lifetimes, is now surfacing for healing and transformation **so we can fully honor and accept our sexuality as part of our spiritual awakening.** This vital integration also helps us to heal the illusion of duality between the physical and spiritual planes that we have accepted as truth in our consciousness.

We are learning to heal the fear surrounding this major energy center. There is so much fear in this area because our sexuality has the power to either heal and create life or, it has the power to make us ill and destroy depending on how we use it. Greed, the power to manipulate and control others, guilt, shame, fear of opening up or contracting a life threatening disease, and perhaps most of all, the unhealed wounds of previous relationships that have damaged our trust in ourselves and each other, have all contributed to blocking our vital life force, as well as denying our right to be fully alive and human.

We have never been taught how to lovingly and openly approach our sexuality, nor encouraged to fully explore its healing potential. This is a subject that really needs major attention in our present human culture and should be taught in all educational systems during puberty – a child's flowering time into adult sexuality. Sexuality is still a "taboo" subject that is not openly and freely integrated into our social and inter-personal life. There are certain topics that are not discussed openly for fear of exposing a personal desire or a sexual preference that may not be socially acceptable. Social labels and limiting projections such as "gay, bisexual, or straight" add to the crystallization (judgments) of belief patterns that block our receiving of unconditional love, in whatever form it may wish to manifest. It is remarkable how much hatred, fear and abuse is generated in humanity as a result of this lack of self-acceptance within each person's sexual identity on this planet. Sigmund Freud had a theory that every child that is born has an intrinsic openness to embrace both the male and female aspect of sexuality. This openness is usually given the word bisexual in our society. I do believe this phenomena to be true of all beings at birth.

What is natural is to love both aspects of ourself. Whether or not both of these aspects are expressed sexually later in life does not take away from the natural expression and healing of our sexual identity. Whether this manifests as sexual intimacy with an opposite sex or the same sex makes absolutely no difference in the openness and value of that intimate experience.

As Corinne Heline clearly expresses in one of her books:

*"Man in the making was bi-sexual. The masculine and feminine polarities, now focused cosmically in the Sun and Moon respectively, exercised an equal influence over the plastic* (malleable, etheric substance) *bodies of early humanity. But this was at a time when the earth and the Moon were still parts of the solar orb. At a later stage when the earth was thrown off from the Sun and, at a still later date, when the Moon was thrown off from the earth, these two polarities ceased to have an equal and balanced expression in individual human beings. Some responded preponderantly to the positive pole centered in the Sun, while others responded to the negative pole focused in the Moon. Eventually, this resulted in the division of humanity into two separate sexes with man and woman appearing upon the scene . ."*
taken from *Music: The Keynote of Human Evolution* by Corinne Heline

Our society is much too obsessed with the judgment and reactive fear of sexual gender identity. Because there is so much resistance and "emotional charge" in so many people regarding this subject, it clearly reveals a part of the self that is "held" in judgment and denial.

There is no such thing as "normal" behavior. Each person's form of sexual expression, desires, fantasies and ideals are all unique and special. There is no standard norm in human sexual behavior that is true and ideal for every person on this planet. What for some is great ecstacy and exciting stimulation is for another revolting and abusive behavior. The important thing is not to deny the emotional fulfillment of your very own sexual expression.

Another important point is not to project our personal sexual identity onto others as a proper form of expression for them. We need to learn to honor each person's unique truth as sacred. Learning to completely accept our own personal sexual preference, whether it is for someone of the opposite sex, or a same-sex relationship is crucial in healing our sexual identity. Whether a person chooses a man or woman makes absolutely no difference in love and self-acceptance. The following information is very beneficial regardless of your sexual orientation, as it will enhance and expand your capacity to receive more loving and vital energy for the healing and transformation of your sexuality identity.

### BALANCING
### THE MALE–FEMALE POLARITIES

On the universal plane, soulmates can manifest as two women or two men or a man and a woman. As the separation between the spirit and flesh is dissolved, we are on our way to healing the illusion of all duality within us. Until our spiritual awareness of love, sexuality and devotion is integrated into the physical, cellular level, we will not have the freedom to function as wholistic beings upon earth. Sexual energy can be observed as pure energy radiating in and out from one center or focal point in the universe. As it expands outwardly, it is projected into the outer world of our experience. We usually identify this **projecting** aspect as the **masculine** aspect. However, the same energy that radiates and projects itself outwardly, returns back to its center and is **absorbed** into the focal point of origin. The energy **returning inwardly** toward the center is considered to be the **feminine** aspect. In reality, however, both this outwardly projecting (male aspect) and inwardly re-absorbing (female aspect) process are truly ONE pulsation of energy occurring simultaneously. THIS IS NOT A DUAL activity. It only appears as such because our mental perception is limited to the projected illusions of duality within the human mind. In reality this phenomenon is totally ONE unified movement of LIFE AND CREATION.

# 3

# OUR SEXUAL IDENTITY

Since our sexual chakra is located between the base of the spine (Primal Fire – Survival) and the solar plexus (Seat of our Emotions), it is easy to understand that there is constantly an interchange between these three centers. All sexual expression has an emotional connection that contains a corresponding desire to experience the primal fire of the physical aspect of our life by becoming one with it. There is a continuous interplay between our emotional needs and feelings seeking expression and their integration within and through our physical body. Our sexuality is the interface between these two energies.

Sexuality helps us 'to get in touch' with the spirit and mystery of the physical plane, that need to touch, to embrace, to be one with, and to heal. There is also a great emotional and physical need for the human being to be able to let go of control and to surrender. This process of 'letting go' and surrendering to love - learning to release control, is very much a part of the sexual drive. If issues of control are not healed, then major issues of power and abuse will manifest themselves within our sexual expression. This is the root of 'sexual abuse'. All sexual abuse stems from denying or holding back a vital essence of our emotional expression. Whether you are the abuser, or abused, the same parallel issues of control and/or denial manifest themselves by not 'allowing' yourself to be loved or not 'accepting' this need within yourself. The subconscious desire to control others through manipulation of sexual power is a result of not feeling good about yourself and, most of all, not knowing how to give and nurture yourself with love. An obsessive need for control sabotages any form of intimacy that may involve the possibility of surrender, opening oneself, and true release.

We can blame all of this on our parental upbringing, environment or our partner. However, if we reclaim our true power and take full responsibility for creating our own reality, we begin to realize that we ourselves chose these particular parents and created whatever emotional pattern, psychological, physical, or sexual abuse that we have encountered in life for our own growth and spiritual evolution. Once we accept this, we can begin to heal the wounds we carry and the bitterness we have felt toward our parents for 'not being there for us', for being over-dominating, over-possessive, non-supportive, or unconsciously projecting their own insecurities upon us as children.

At some point before each being incarnated, a specific life-plan was chosen by us to include an agenda of challenges to heal any form of self-abuse or abuse-to-others. The abuse may have started ten thousand years ago in a far distant lifetime. If the cause and pattern of that abuse has not been recognized and healed, the pattern will re-enact itself over and over again during each lifetime until the cause of the abusive pattern is recognized, released, transformed and healed. In blaming others, we only procrastinate and 'put off' our own healing process and release of that blocked energy. The same emotional or sexual patterns will continually repeat themselves until the increasing discomfort and pain forces us to take a vital step forward to healing these abusive patterns within ourselves.

When we are terrified of our own vulnerability, it will effect how receptive and expressive we are sexually. If we 'hold back', there is usually a major pattern of sexual manipulation to be resolved; we will feel like someone is abusing us. When we begin to practice 'feeling good about ourselves', fully accepting and appreciating our own personal sexuality, and learning to trust all parts of ourselves, we then begin to reclaim our own power and identity. Once we fully trust ourselves, no one will ever be able to manipulate or abuse us in any way. Become aware of your own inner space. Accepting full responsibility for the creation of your own reality frees you from the 'clutches' of the victim syndrome and any form of control or abuse by others. No one else is going to accept you, if you don't accept yourself. If you don't feel good about your own sexuality, it will be mirrored back to you through an intimate partner. A lot of people in our culture are terrified of intimacy because of the fear of rejection and other forms of abuse. This great fear of being open and vulnerable runs rampant in our society, as issues of trust have been so abused in modern relationships. We really do have some major healing to do in the department of trust, intimacy, sexuality and vulnerability. This goes for almost every single human being on the planet at this present time.

As the patriarchal hierarchy begins to crumble and dissolve, old, dysfunctional patterns of male dominated institutions and values are also undergoing a major planetary transformation. The reason that so many women have stepped into their own power is to reclaim the freedom and willpower of their own inner male polarity in a more positive, loving, creative and life-supporting way. Because of so much abuse in the old patriarchal system, women have pulled away from these abusive patterns to find their own inner balance, freedom and integrity, and to reclaim the total respect and same recognition that men have enjoyed. Naturally there is a tremendous re-polarization taking place within both sexes at the present time. The very basic issue that now confronts each man and each woman is how to bring both aspects of the male and female polarity into integration and a harmonious balance.

There really is a big sexual revolution going on right now, as old role patterns are dissolving and each of us is learning to find a new, more healing and fulfilling pattern of relationship and sexual identity. Once each man and woman finds the natural balance and harmony between the male and female polarity within themselves (by healing any emotional issues or abuse that we have experienced with our mother and father) any issues of control, domination, lack of acceptance, etc. will no longer exist in relationship to the many layers and expressions of human intimacy. Once we truly feel okay about the male and female energy in each of us, we will not be obsessed with any issues about sexual gender preference. At this very moment, if everyone 'came out of the closet' and stood 'naked and exposed' in their unique sexual orientation, it would truly facilitate major sexual self-acceptance and healing on the planet. It is the 'hiding' from ourselves, not just from others, that creates conflict, tension and disease. As we assume full responsibility for the acceptance and healing of our own sexuality, the door will open for society to heal itself of its own judgments and fears.

There has long been too much emphasis and focus in our society and the media about the 'perfect' male or the 'sexy' female role model. This has truly diverted us from accepting and nurturing our own inner beauty, truth and unique personal identity. There is no formula for love or 'sexiness' that will attract everyone. We cannot deny the beauty of our own individual uniqueness and 'persona'. It's the spark of light within our own inner heart that really makes us attractive. Remove the individual 'persona' and you have a robot doll. The challenge is to practice 'honesty' in your process of sexual healing and awareness. Allow whatever fears, insecurities and old pains you have to surface so you can experience these feelings in-depth. As they surface, you can practice the same seven-step recovery program as the one used for emotional abuse (See page 50). Recognizing your true feelings and allowing them to be openly and fully expressed releases many patterns of abuse as well as accumulated physical tension. This process in turn creates the space for a new pattern of self-healing to manifest with tender, loving care and self nurturing.

THE ESSENCE OF OUR EVOLVING SEXUALITY REALLY EXPRESSES AN INTRINSIC DESIRE FOR UNION WITH GOD, a Union with the Source of All Life, to feel yourself reabsorbed into the ONE. This is the ecstasy for which each one of us longs; this is the ecstasy that each one of us can have.

# 4

# A GUIDED MEDITATION
# TO ENHANCE
# OUR SEXUAL EXPRESSION

This meditation exercise can be done with or without a partner and in whatever manner of clothing you are most comfortable, as your attention and energy is being channeled through your creative, inner visualization. If you don't have a partner, you can do this same, wonderful meditation attunement by visualizing the man or woman of your choice sitting together with you in the straddling tantric meditation posture, much like the classic Far Eastern tantric deities. As you face each other, your bodies touch and embrace one another. The whole point of this meditation exercise is to allow the vital life force energy of the sexual center to flow freely by rising throughout the entire body and energy centers (chakras) without physical, sexual intercourse. Begin by putting on some healing music, light a candle and prepare a quiet space where you, and if applicable your partner, can be undisturbed for about 45 minutes. I highly recommend playing *CRYSTAL ILLUMINATION* (See Appendix) as this album was designed to activate and fine-tune the chakras.

First, you and your partner sit apart facing each other. (You may want to use a pillow to aid you into a comfortable sitting posture so your spine can be erect with minimal physical strain.) Begin by breathing deeply and slowly until both of you find a simultaneous rhythm of breathing together slowly and evenly. Now, continue with with the four-cycle breathing exercise (See page 5) as you silently affirm within for each breath cycle the following:

as you inhale, affirm
"I AM INBREATHING GOD'S LOVE INTO MY ETHERIC BODY"

as you hold your breath, affirm
"I AM ABSORBING GOD'S LOVE INTO MY MENTAL BODY"

as you begin to slowly exhale, affirm
"I AM EXPANDING GOD'S LOVE IN MY EMOTIONAL BODY"

hold your exhalation as you affirm
"I AM PROJECTING GOD'S LOVE INTO MY PHYSICAL BODY".

Do this four cycle breathing for about two to three minutes until your breathing rhythm becomes synchronized.

When you feel ready and relaxed, both you and your partner move closer together into the classic, embracing tantric position with one partner straddling the other. Your bodies are now touching and facing one another. If you like, your hands can rest gently on your lap with palms up; or, if you prefer, around your partner's waist or hips. Continue breathing slowly and deeply. (It will help to keep your eyes closed during the entire meditation.)

Bring your attention to the base of your spine. Visualize a column of white light connecting your base chakra with the base chakra of your partner. Feel the wonderful sensation and flow through the interconnecting beam of white light from your partner's center to yours. Feel your base center opening gradually, expanding to receive the energy and vibration of your partner's base chakra through this radiant column of white light connecting you through the white ray of purity. Don't hold back any sensations or feelings in that area; simply learn to let go and become receptive to one another. This exercise focuses on "receiving" rather than sending or projecting energy consciously. The energy will flow naturally of itself if you allow yourself to receive and visualize this mutual interchange of energy and light.

After three to five minutes of visualizing this opening and receiving at the base of your spine, move on to the sacrum center. This is the seat of your sexuality. Visualize a column of brilliant violet light connecting your vital sexual center with your partner's. Feel the opening of your sexual center as you receive this beautiful violet light from your partner unfolding, opening and gently massaging your sexual center. You feel completely safe as you release all effort and receive the warmth and comfort that is radiating through this violet tube of light. As you receive this radiance from your partner, visualize your sexuality becoming completely open and free in expression. Release all tension in that area and any constriction or pain that you might be internalizing. Allow the violet light to transmute and dissolve any blocks or obstructions in your sexual center. During this transmuting process, breathe the violet light into and out from this vital energy center. Experience the wonderful sensations of mutual interchange in this area between you and your partner.

Again, after three to five minutes (you may want to expand the meditation at the sacrum center for a longer period, as most of us need greater healing in this area) move your attention up into your solar plexus, your emotional center. Visualize a ruby-golden column of light joining you and your partner in the abdomen area. Breathe in the ruby-golden light into your solar plexus. As you breathe in this light, allow any tension in that area to dissolve upon exhaling. As you inbreathe ruby light, exhale golden light. Feel the power of this emotional center opening itself like a warm, radiant sun. Now visualize a beam of ruby-violet connecting your emotional centers, creating a space of safety and peace. Feel the warmth and nurturing of these two suns connecting and interpenetrating each other, creating greater light, warmth and inner nurturing. (You may wish to focus on this center a bit longer as well if you need more emotional healing.)

When you feel ready, slowly bring your focus into your heart center. Breathe in pink light into your heart and breathe out white light for about two minutes. Visualize a brilliant, pink column of light connecting your heart with your partner's heart center. As you breathe the pink light into your heart, focus on receiving this pink light from your partner's heart center through the beam of pink light connecting you. Do not effort anything; just simply allow your heart center to slowly open, receive and connect with your partner in a glorious pink radiance. Feel your heart center opening as you visualize a soft golden-pink rose unfolding its petals. Breathe in the tender, glowing pink light and breathe out radiant golden light. As your inter-connection deepens, you may want to visualize irridescent sparks of rainbow light emitting from the column of pink light as your love connection expands. When you have absorbed to overflowing the pink light, allow this color and frequency to run joyously throughout your whole body. Feel it in your head, throat, your arms, hands, chest, abdomen, spine, genitals, legs, and feet. Feel your whole body absorbing this pink, diamond light essence until you feel totally comforted and embraced by this love ray.

When you feel ready, move up into your throat center and breathe in a wonderful cobalt blue light. Feel your throat center opening out into a brilliant column of cobalt blue light connecting your throat center with the throat chakra of your partner. Allow yourself to receive the energy pulsation of your partner through this blue beam of light. Breathe in blue light into your throat and exhale blue light as you slowly release your breath. Do this attunement for approximately five to seven minutes. Keep your focus on the beam of blue light connecting you, as your throat center opens wide to receive the cobalt blue ray.

Slowly bring your attention up into your third eye center (the center place on the forehead between your eyebrows). Visualize a deep indigo beam of light connecting this center with your partner's. As you focus on your third eye, you see a column of indigo light moving back and forth between you and your partner. Visualize this beam of indigo light turning into emerald green as the rate of light vibration uniting you accelerates. The rate of pulsation in your third eye increases and changes into emerald green as the light in your third eye expands and opens this center of healing and extra-sensory perception. Feel the strobing pattern of light spiraling in and through your third eye center as it begins opening. Continue breathing slowly and deeply. Now, just focus on pure white, golden light flowing between your united third eye centers, and feel the activation and opening of that center. Just sit very still for a time experiencing this wonderful sensation of light as you absorb its healing essence.

Now bring your attention into your crown chakra at the very top-center of your head. Breathe in a glorious, splendid golden light. As you sustain and hold your inhalation, ABSORB this golden light into your entire head area and brain cells. Exhale golden light and repeat this breathing process for a couple of minutes. Now visualize an arch of golden light connecting your open crown with your partner's open crown. It's like a rainbow bridge of light connecting the top of both of your heads in a beam of golden, radiant light. Feel this golden radiance penetrate all the way down through a column of white light within you and into every part of your body filling your aura with a golden glow of illumination. As you receive this inflow of golden liquid light from the arched beam of light above your crown, both you and your partner's crown centers are completely open to one another, as your life's purpose, aspirations and visions are in complete alignment with higher Universal Intelligence and God's Will. Your crown is your trans-personal receiving station that is now being activated as you prepare for the next step.

As you inbreathe this golden light from your crown center, the golden arch slowly turns into a bright rainbow arch of light. All the colors of the rainbow begin to enter your crown center. As this rainbow light is entering through the crown of your head, it flows through the column of white light into each chakra: through the third eye, moving down into your throat center, your heart, solar plexus, sacrum, and base of your spine. As the rainbow light touches the base of your spine it immediately connects and flows into the base of the spine of your partner, then moves up into the sacrum, solar plexus and up into your partner's heart, throat area, third eye and crown center. As the rainbow light moves up into the crown center of your partner, it flows out through the arched rainbow and back into your crown, all the way down into your base center, then immediately flows into your partner's base of the spine center, then upwards and back and forth like a wheel of rainbow light. Simply sit and experience the ecstatic, blissful union of rainbow light that is being generated back and forth between the two of you. (At a certain time during this interchange process, you may want to reverse the flow of this circular energy from counter-clockwise to clockwise.) Your whole body is absorbing the healing rainbow colors as all your energy centers are now re-vitalizing and flowing in complete alignment with your partner's.

Breathe in rainbow light into your crown and exhale white light. Then alternate by inbreathing white light and exhaling rainbow light. Your whole body is re-charged, re-balanced and in harmonic alignment with your tantric partner. When you feel complete in this attunement, embrace your partner, and if you feel like it, kiss one another as you share pure rainbow love.

# 5

## HEALING SEXUAL ABUSE

For healing any form of sexual abuse it is helpful to go through the following preliminary steps for self-healing:

1.  'Get in touch' with your feelings and emotions.

2.  Do not invalidate your experience by judging it as 'wrong or 'bad'. Do not judge yourself for drawing this experience into your life.

3.  See this experience as an opportunity for completely re-claiming your power, self-worth, and freedom.

4.  Do not judge or blame the abuser.   Do not judge or blame yourself.

5.  Call upon the Violet, transmuting Flame (See page 147), beloved St. Germain, and follow through with the guided meditation and visualization for the violet ray.

6. Follow the same seven-step recovery program as used for emotional abuse. (See page 50)

This is a great opportunity to heal all patterns of 'being a victim', 'projecting blame' and externalizing our anger onto someone else. As you reclaim your full power and responsibility, there is not even a chance that you will ever attract such a painful mirror again.

# PART II

# HEALING OUR
# EMOTIONAL BODY

# 6

# NURTURING AND HEALING OUR EMOTIONS:
## CARING FOR OUR INNER CHILD

This area of our being is perhaps the most turbulent and misunderstood phenomenon of all. Since we cannot rely on just rationality and logic in our lives, this part of ourself keeps surfacing to facilitate great shifts of energy-growth-expansion within our being. When we experience a state of contraction, we feel pain and therefore long to be in a less constrictive state of being. We feel imprisoned by our own lack of clarity, insight, or our powerlessness to change or shift those feelings or emotions that are screaming out at us for attention.

The first stage of healing our emotional body is to know more about the area in which our emotions surface and express themselves, as well as where and how they 'get stuck'. It is very helpful for us to know and get acquainted with that area in our solar plexus (the abdomen area) where these raw emotions surface for processing. One of the main functions of this center is a self-automatic, protection program. All of us have experienced feelings of defensiveness when we are 'being attacked'. This is one of the primary reflexes of the solar plexus chakra:  to protect, guard and support our well-being.  It is also the area of the digestive tract, whose purpose is to assimilate and absorb the necessary life force to keep us alive and healthy.

Throughout time, the basic life-love force essence of humanity has been so suppressed that great amounts of energy have become blocked and trapped in the emotional center of our being.  That is why so many people cannot even move or function in relationships and life without experiencing some emotional pain and therefore, cannot move with ease into the higher centers of the heart, throat, third-eye and crown.  For the past 30 years, many beings on the spiritual path have focused on developing the higher chakras without completing the clearing, transmutation, and healing of the first three energy centers.  In many cases, religion and spirituality became an addiction in order to escape from the 'unpleasant', erratic, uncomfortable parts of our self that were not ready to be dealt with or exposed.  The main reason for this was that we had no effective training or education in how to relate wholistically to these basic human emotional issues without self-judgment for those greatly misunderstood feelings and emotions.  What the spiritual focus has done to many seekers, those who have not completed the clearing and healing process in the first three chakras, is to precipitate and accelerate a polarization of energy that brings to the surface all areas and parts of ourselves that we have not loved, denied, judged, suppressed or feared seeing.  As the pain surfaces more often, at times unbearably, we feel as if we may  just "snap".  During such a critical time of emotional crisis we have several choices:

1.  We can choose to block out the pain, and try to es-
    cape by some form of reactive-addictive and co-
    dependent behavior, such as: alcohol, drug use,
    sex, rescuing and healing others, becoming work-
    oholics, basically anything that diverts our atten-
    tion or focus away from the pain of having to face
    a part of ourselves that makes us feel un-
    comfortable.

2.  We may ask for spiritual guidance or support, go
    to someone for counseling, or seek the advice of a
    psychic or spiritual teacher. However, this can
    also become an additive behavior pattern.

3.  Or, we may choose to lovingly surrender self-
    resistance and RECOGNIZE that there is something
    we have denied for so long, something we have
    been afraid to see, something that has created a
    blockage and 'gotten stuck' within us. The first
    healthy stage **of the clearing and healing** process
    is **RECOGNITION.** Recognition is awareness. How-
    ever, this does not mean that just being aware or
    recognizing a problem will in any way solve it.

4.  The second stage following recognition is ACCEP-
    TANCE. We accept the fact that there is something
    within US that is out of balance or alignment,
    something that is blocking the flow of our vital life
    energy. **ACCEPTANCE WITHOUT JUDGMENT is** the
    key. It is the first step in approaching the process
    of self-transformation. What is self-acceptance
    without judgment? It means "shifting into neutral
    gear" and assuming a neutral, "observing" van-
    tage point in which you are able to witness with

love and compassion that part of yourself that is suffering. As you witness these emotions and feelings, you learn compassion toward yourself by not judging or condemning yourself as being 'wrong' for any feeling you are experiencing, whether it is anger, jealousy, fear, greed, lust, envy, rejection, issues of self-worth, or any form of denial or repression. This is the stage where most of us "get stuck" and are not able to move beyond this level to the next stage.

Let's take a closer look at why it is so difficult for us not to condemn ourselves, or why we judge so many feelings negatively, as 'disgusting' or have thoughts like "I should be beyond this; this is not part of me; I just don't want to see it, so the less energy I give it, the less power it has over me". This last attitude is also a great stumbling block; it creates increased resistance and fear as it suppresses the emotions even more, creating 'self-sabotage' as the inner pain becomes intolerable. How can we love ourselves, when the whole world around us judges us for feeling angry, hurt, being "out of control", not fitting into the 'norm' of standard social acceptability? A great weakness of many therapies has been to negatively judge these basic human emotions and deny their expression because they are seen as "negative, dirty, destructive and poison". Anything that will eliminate these "spiritually unevolved" emotions, (that we all feel and possess), is immediately acceptable and our search for escape grows even greater.

There is a song by Yoko Ono that perceives these basic human emotions from a very different and more positive perspective. Here is an excerpt from her album *SKY PEOPLE:*

*"Bless you for your anger, it's a sign of 'rising energy'. Direct not to your enemy, direct not to yourself. If you turn it into love, it will bring you happiness. Bless you for your anger, it's a sign of 'rising energy'." "Bless you for your greed, it's a sign of 'great capacity', etc. ."*

**The key to our transformation and our movement into that transformation is HOW we perceive, relate to, and respond to the "raw data" or unqualified energy of our basic human emotions before any 'reaction' takes over.** That is what is meant by "shifting into neutral gear"; learning to distance ourselves from our own reactive, emotional process in order to be more loving and compassionate with our own self. This means that we do not have to buy into the illusion of our limited perceptions that energize a dual-oriented, conditioned, emotional pattern. This polarization of duality within the mind creates a 'split' in our consciousness, as we are torn between conflicting patterns of information. We simply learn to witness and to observe our emotional process with more love and compassion. Understanding how we function as human beings, and integrating the "connecting links" of self-love, compassion and witness into our healing process, are the seeds for our transformation. What are some of the other inter-connecting links for our emotional healing?

RAW DATA IS JUST THAT, RAW INFORMATION THAT HAS NOT BEEN ENCODED WITH A VALUE JUDGEMENT. It is simply there for us to see and observe. It's not so much even a matter of learning to be objective with ourselves, as even that can still be a trap of dual-oriented thinking which can create the polarization and separation between subject and object. **It's more a matter of allowing**

**ourselves the experience to observe and witness our own human creation without judging it as either 'right or wrong', 'good or bad.'** The ability and freedom to just view the emotion (without suppressing it) as a neutral observer is truly learning the art of detachment. Once we have practiced this 'viewing' process and integrated this awareness and acceptance into our healing process, we will truly be on our way to a healthier and happier life.

Judging ourselves as 'bad' or 'wrong' for experiencing certain feelings is a form of self-condemnation that energizes an inherent belief "I DON'T DESERVE LOVE", or "I AM NOT WORTHY OF BEING LOVED IF THESE FEELINGS KEEP COMING UP." This attitude is what keeps us "locked" into a defensive mode of emotional reaction that stifles our development until the time when we learn to shift our perception and awareness to a greater degree of self-acceptance without self-judgment or self-punishment. "Yes, I can still have anger, experience hurt, and yes, I can still be loved; I still deserve love. Being angry does not mean that I don't love myself. I don't have to punish myself for having and experiencing these emotions." Many emotional expressions and reactions show themselves like a child who has been ignored, one who is screaming out for attention in need of something that he or she is not getting. It is when we ignore that call of the innocent child, who does not distinguish between good and evil, right or wrong, that we begin to block our own life force, which then, in turn, manifests in some form of imbalance mentally, emotionally, physically, or at times, all three.

When a child is forbidden to act, it seeks to do the very thing which is forbidden; because a child does not comprehend limits or boundaries, it seeks to explore the why's of "no, no". Part of the child is daring, wanting to discover for itself the hidden, forbidden territory that is being denied. The emotions that we have been taught to suppress or deny as children react in much the same way. When an emotion or a strong feeling is projected unto the child by the parents as 'unacceptable', the child automatically withdraws into a self-protective shell (in the solar plexus) and internalizes the emotional denial. This denial eventually crystallizes into a fear or blockage in that area especially if these emotions are not encouraged to be expressed, explored and handled without judgment or punishment. The emotional responses of many children continue to re-enact a psychological behavior pattern that perpetuates the very experience which has been forbidden, denied, or judged. If left unattended, these same forbidden feelings and emotions will resurface in our adult relationships and in our career, until we heal the abuse and judgment connected with that emotional experience. It's a question of giving ourselves permission to look into areas of ourselves that we have never been encouraged to explore, much less accept. Our parents' fears and denial patterns unconsciously projected themselves into our emotional body during our childhood and many times we absorbed these judgements and fears into our subconscious like a sponge.

For our healing, what we learn to do later in life is to literally 're-parent' our childhood, and re-pattern our feeling world by giving ourselves full permission to explore those hidden, forbidden regions of ourselves that were held previously in denial, judgement, and fear. This is why it is so important not to judge ourselves for having any repressed emotions, as judgment creates an even greater barrier and separation between ourselves and the abuse within us which we hope to heal. Judgment is an emotional reaction of shame, fear, resistance, and separation. It is a statement of non-acceptance. Judgment is rejection in action. When we judge another, we are actually rejecting a part of ourselves that we do not accept. So we skillfully arrange distancing maneuvers to separate ourselves from that which, through others, we do not wish to see in ourselves. This is where the human arena of 'personal projections' begin to manifest, as we project our own personal pain, and lack of self-acceptance onto others. This is precisely our perdicament, and as a consequence, human relationships suffer.

When someone approaches us that sparks those feelings within our emotional body that are still in denial and judgment, our emotional reaction sets up an automatic 'defense mechanism' that takes over and rises up like a shield. To the degree in which those emotions or feelings have not been loved, accepted, or healed, we will unconsciously 'project' our lack of self-acceptance onto others. Naturally this creates a major communication gap, as sharing is not only mental, but involves many feelings of the heart, and sharing brings us consequently to the very important and intimate healing issue of TRUST. Within the process of projecting our own unhealed emotions onto others, we automatically set up the same pattern of 'judgment' that we hold over ourselves onto the other person. **Any unhealed pattern of self-judgment will automatically translate itself into a projection of judgment onto others.** One can now see the importance of our own emotional self-acceptance and healing as a prerequisite to creating healthy, loving relationships.

# 7

# HEALING THE ILLUSION OF DUALITY IN OUR EMOTIONS

Emotions = Energy in Motion; it is neither good nor bad, positive nor negative. It is just movement letting itself be known, letting us know what we are holding back, what we are acknowledging in ourselves and others, it lets us know when we are loving or acting out of fear. When issues of fear, anger, jealousy or possessiveness surface, immediately "take a step back", "shift into neutral", and become a witness of your emotions by observing the effect they have on you.

Find a quiet place where you can just sit without being disturbed, and allow whatever you are feeling to surface and manifest itself. Make a commitment as you "step back" NOT to project this emotional state onto your lover, yourself, or whatever other person it involves. Make a commitment not to judge your emotion as negative, bad, or "lower than your higher self". If feelings of shame come up, ask yourself what part of yourself you are not loving? Then acknowledge to yourself that the feeling that is surfacing is really a blessing in disguise, because it wants to show you something about yourself that wants more love, attention, acceptance, and nurturing. What part of yourself have you held back, that such a strong emotional expression is surfacing? Embrace the feeling, the tears, the helplessness. In this quiet place, re-parent your emotional pattern, by VALIDATING whatever it is you're feeling with unconditional love and self-acceptance. In a warm, tender embrace, hold your inner self and your inner pain in loving safety; allow the mother-nurturer in you to manifest by creating a conducive, healing environment where you can let go of all defenses; where you can allow yourself to be the child again. Allow yourself to feel your hurt, letting go of all resistance. Allow the tears to flow; allow any emotions that want to be expressed to manifest. Take a moment to validate your pain, acknowledge its existence, then ask yourself: (Cross reference page 52, Step 4) "Pain, anger, frustration, (name whatever other emotion is surfacing), please show yourself to me, so that I can see and become aware of what is creating you inside of me; show me what part of myself I have not been acknowledging, loving, recognizing, or accepting. Beloved Holy Spirit, I open myself to a total healing of the cause, effect, record, and memory of this part of myself that I have not loved, until there is a total acceptance, understanding, and healing of my whole self."

Now, go deeper within. Continue to 'mother' your pain and your feelings by visualizing soft white light around yourself, around your tender, loving body. Allow your heart to fill with that soft golden-white light and continue to embrace the pain and hurt by visualizing it as an infant or small child. You are actually allowing your inner child to be loved, cared for, and embraced in unconditional love. You can acknowledge your inner child by saying: **"I am totally here for you. I love you. I will never leave you."** Continue visualizing the soft white light spreading waves of compassion around your inner child, and keep affirming the above words to yourself and to your inner child. Within a short time, you will begin to experience a softening of those emotions, and you will feel a gradual easing of the energy blocked within you. What we are really healing here or anywhere, at any time, is the healing of self-ignorance. When we are open to observing ourselves in a neutral mode, becoming more and more aware and perceptive, at that point we begin 'to know' and see. Ignorance is the absence of knowing, the absence of awareness. It is the part of ourselves that we have not been willing to see whether consciously or unconsciously, for whatever reason. We must first heal the fear that confronts us as we begin to acknowledge a part of ourselves that we have been afraid to see, love and accept. Some of us simply block out certain memories because they are too painful, or because we feel that we might loose control, or that "our safe little bubble might burst". One important affirmation that may be used during this opening process is to say to yourself silently (or out loud): "I _____, now create a space of safety, a loving place of support and nurturing for my inner Self, as I build my bridge from a state of fear, to a state of TRUST."

During this process of nurturing and clearing, it is very important not to ignore ANY feelings that may arise. This is a golden opportunity and time for surrender, a time to allow your inner child to speak and express itself fully to you. During this phase of giving your inner child all the love, support and attention it needs, you are at the same time giving birth to a child that is happier, more fulfilled and more secure. The process of re-parenting your inner child is a continuous journey through many layers in our emotional body that need acknowledgment, acceptance and healing. Allow yourself more time to retreat into your own inner space by creating a safe environment to re-parent your inner child. As you do so, you will notice a new "YOU" emerging that is stronger, healthier and more free. You will also observe how your relationship to children and others around you will change. Once again, one of the most important things to remember is not to judge your inner child for all or any of its feelings, emotions, outbursts, etcs. Instead, learn to GIVE greater love, approval and acceptance to that part of yourself.

When you are in the process of creative visualization, I highly suggest playing a selection of healing music, such as *ANGEL LOVE* or *MAJESTY* (See Appendix). As you begin to feel the warm, soft golden-light radiating throughout you, visualize it emanating from your heart and surrounding your inner child. You may want to put a pyramid of white light around yourself. This pyramid of light will be your shield of protection during your healing process, and at the same time, it will strengthen, accelerate and amplify all the loving energy you are radiating for the healing of your inner child. As the golden-white light around your inner child begins to grow, you may also visualize the pyramid expanding in radiance until it fills the  room . . the house . . . the town . . . the planet. You are now creating a field of resonance that will attract and magnetize the universal healing essence that you need. Not only does this benefit you, but the entire environment in which you live and work, your family, friends, and associates. When you no longer encounter any resistance or contraction within you, then you are well on your  way to releasing the old dysfunctional patterns of abuse in the emotional body. Work on healing one issue at a time. Pace yourself; be gentle. It is better to move slowly and more thoroughly than to try to "take on" too much, too fast. As you begin to make progress in your self-healing,  you will realize that you have the power, ability and authority to dissolve any constricting patterns of identity within your life. Once you realize that you are the creator of your own pain, suffering and in fact, all of your life experiences, you are then able to use that same creative power to manifest a you that is free from pain, suffering, abuse and delusion.

Creation is a regenerative process. We can always change, dissolve, restructure, or transmute any belief system which contributed to the creation and manifestation of our present reality. What no longer works can be discarded as obsolete. New areas of self-exploration are born to serve a more expanded and integrated self. Creation is always in flux, ever-changing; it is mutable. It is the same with the self; it grows, dissolves and discards old ego patterns. It experiences death and dying as a form of releasing the ego from limited, constricted areas of identification. Death and dying, whether on the physical or mental-emotional plane is only an accelerated release of a self that has outlived the tremendous strain of constriction, pain and the inability to move beyond our own human creation. There are many ways in which we can transmute and shift our old patterns without having to go through the death and dying experience. Once we realize how near a part of ourselves is to dying, we can then begin to work on ourselves in a more healthy, self-loving way to release the old pattern that will bypass the potentially extreme physical, mental or emotional trauma. Usually, the three are always connected. Many people choose illness as a form to release old abusive patterns and emotional blocks, as it brings us closer to the critical point between life and death. We must choose either to release the cause of the affliction through consciously facing the abusive pattern by healing it, or in extreme cases to release it through physical death. Each of us has the power of choice in life. Ultimately it is only ourselves that chooses which form of 'release' will manifest to help us evolve into a more integrated, wholistic SELF.

# 8

# ISSUES OF ABANDONMENT
# AND REJECTION

During our lifetime, many of us have experienced various forms of rejection, abandonment and unrequited
love. This is a very important issue in our human development, especially during the formative years of our
childhood. Many of us have experienced some form of
grief through loss or abandonment such as being an
'unwanted' child, having parents divorce or separate
during our early childhood, or having a parent die or
become seriously ill. At such times, we experienced a
great loss; that loss translates itself into abandonment;
we feel all alone and empty inside; we feel unloved and
defenseless. It is also during these young formative years
that the belief begins to crystallize that "no one really
loves me or is there for me; I am not deserving of love; I
am a victim." Once again this sets up a chain reaction of
circumstances that will repeat themselves in life through
all kinds of relationships, especially intimate ones, situations where we re-experience rejection and abandonment over and over, until we heal the original pattern and
cause of any love, attention, and validation that was
denied us during our childhood. Why do we deny
ourselves the love we so much want and need? Why do

we deny receiving the love that others want to give us? To answer these questions in a nutshell, one of the greatest lessons for all souls incarnating upon this earth is to learn complete self-love, self-forgiveness, and self-acknowledgement through expanding our awareness of who we are as an essential, complete soul entity. For most people on earth, one of the largest missing links is the lack of understanding and acknowledgement of our spiritual origin, or the soul aspect of our existence. There is a great denial in this area of spiritual awareness as the mind and desires are preoccupied with material accomplishment and achievement. Naturally this greatly affects all our relationships as the denial is mirrored in all of our intimate, as well as external interactions in the world.

Many spiritually evolved souls also hold the subconscious belief that they have been abandoned from their spiritual origins when taking birth here on earth. This is also a very major issue for a lot of lightworkers today. To help heal this split or separation, we need to acknowledge within ourselves that each of us made a conscious choice to come here. By consciously re-affirming our complete responsibility for making that choice, we can begin to heal the illusion of separation and abandonment that we have accepted emotionally, mentally and spiritually as we took human birth. One of the reasons so many souls choose an earth incarnation is because all the challenges act as a catalyst to accelerate the process of our personal and spiritual evolution more quickly than on other planets. Earth is similar to a "launching pad" where one can make great spiritual progress and move directly into higher dimensions once our lessons are completed here on earth, and thus, bypassing other intermediate, astral learning planes.

# 9

# HEALING EMOTIONAL SELF-ABUSE

The key that opens the door to our desired transformation is through our conscious commitment and acceptance to take full responsibility for all our perceptions
and life experiences. The realization that we have chosen
these experiences for our own evolution rather than as a
form of punishment, accelerates the process of self transformation and healing. There is so much focus today on
child abuse, and how many of us have been 'abused'
either by a relative or a stranger. The words **dysfunctional, co-dependent, abuse, and addiction** are all words
that we see repeatedly in almost all self-help manuals and
psychological therapies. Of all these topics and issues,
however, there is an essential one that is not discussed or
studied in depth. This is the topic of how we create and
act out various forms of **self-abuse.**

Many people that are now "coming out of the closet"
admitting that they were sexually, physically, mentally,
or emotionally abused are unconsciously re-creating the
role of victim: "Look what's been done to me, how I was
abused". Did you ever have the courage to ask yourself
"what part of me created this abusive experience?", what
part of me was I not loving to attract such an intense
experience? What part of myself have I abused to manifest this lack of love in the physical plane? How does

self-abuse start? What is the cause? How can I heal all forms of self-abuse?

WHAT IS SELF-ABUSE? All self-abuse has its roots in denial and repression of our basic human need for love, to be vulnerable, and to receive love. Self-abuse started many lifetimes ago. **There is not one person on this planet who is not, through one form or another, healing a major aspect of self-abuse.** We incarnate on this planet to heal major issues of self-abuse. Whether this started on another planet in another time dimension, or another lifetime here on earth, it does not matter. The point is that as human beings we are all dealing with this same basic issue; we all are learning how to be more loving to ourselves by forgiving, releasing and transmuting the cause, effect and memory of that abuse.

WE CHOOSE OTHERS (PARENTS, ETC.) TO PHYSICALLY, SEXUALLY, EMOTIONALLY OR MENTALLY ACT OUT OUR OWN UNCONSCIOUS FORMS OF SELF-ABUSE. Taking **responsibility** for the cause of this unconscious choice allows us to initiate the first step of our healing and transformation. Self-abuse is a form of self-punishment that goes way back in time, perhaps lifetimes, or even light year dimensions away, when we first had our experience of separation, duality, conflict and pain. Many patterns and forms of abuse that manifest during our childhood, can be karmic "paybacks" from other life times of abuse in which we all participated as human beings. We chose a mother or father (who may have been our lover, business associate, or rival in another lifetime) to act out a form of self-punishment because we have not forgiven or released our own guilt or self-judgment for an experience we participated in when *we* may have been the 'villain' or the abuser in that lifetime.

Self-abuse can also start from unrequited love, abandonment, or rejection in early childhood. Many times
when we do not receive something we really need or
want, or when something dear to us is taken away we feel
cheated and rejected by the universe. Our inner child
screams out in longing and doesn't understand why it
can't have what it needs. Frustration and conflict manifest, and feelings of unworthiness start to creep into the
subconscious mind. This starts a chain of emotional
reactions that inhibit the creative flow of life within us,
and what we really desire in life becomes even more
inaccessible and remote. Somewhere during this succession of events, the thought or belief that "I can never have
this in my life", "I'll never be able to achieve this kind of
success and relationship", or "I'm not good enough"
begin to take over in the subconscious mind. We begin to
feel emotionally paralyzed, our power to move beyond
that thought pattern, beyond that belief is frozen in self -
doubt and fear. **Self-abuse begins at that moment in our
belief system when we have lost the faith both in
ourselves and in the universe to create all that we need
for our happiness and fulfillment.** If we can't create this
fulfillment on earth, how are we going to find it somewhere else? The search starts and ends within your SELF.
No one else holds that key; not a mother, a father, not
your lover, husband or wife. Only you and your God Self
can open the door to love and freedom.

Self-abuse is also a denial of some part of ourselves
that we choose to ignore, a vital part of ourselves that is
not seen as attractive, loved, or accepted into our reality.
Whether it is the spiritual awareness of our God Self, our
sexuality, the quality of our life, the belief in oneself and
life, jealousy, anger, or whatever other aspect of the Self

we are choosing to ignore or deny. This is the very part of us that will create a chain of circumstances and events that will challenge us to eventually face all parts of our being. It truly necessitates learning compassion and tenderness towards our own Self, as we release major patterns of self-judgment, self-punishment, and guilt. We will continue to create situations and experiences in life that are abrasive and painful over and over again, until we finally see and understand with our heart and mind what we are creating. This motivates us to heal the cause and effect of all forms of self-abuse.

As human beings, when we don't receive what we need, we "shut off", feel rejected, worthless, and our faith in our own power crumbles. We immediately feel guilt that "I did something wrong, so I don't feel worthy to receive the love or joy I want." When we entertain this attitude, we begin to feel that "I don't deserve". Our own value of ourselves diminishes to a powerless and helpless creature. THAT IS SELF-ABUSE. Punishing ourselves for "doing something wrong" is also a form of self-abuse. Denying self awareness and holding back the recognition of our deepest feelings, longing and sexual desires, is also a form of self-abuse. **We probably live in one of the most self-abusive societies in the world, where repression, denial, self-punishment and guilt have all contributed to what is called a 'normal, healthy society'.** By starting with ourselves, and healing our own issues of self-abuse, we can contribute to the healing of a humanity in great need of awakening, transformation and wholeness.

# 10

## THE SEVEN STEP RECOVERY PROGRAM
## FOR HEALING EMOTIONAL ABUSE

The most important step in re-claiming your power is to affirm that there is no separation between your human Self and your Divine "I AM" God Presence. (See page 118 for explanation.) If you have problems with self-esteem, this acknowledgement will help you to anchor your God Presence fully into all areas of your being. This includes the mind, your emotions, sexuality, and in general, how you see and relate to yourself. The key is to transmute the old "worn-out" ways of seeing yourself as a 'victim' and a limited being by taking complete charge of your life and reclaiming your true essence and spiritual identity as a conscious-living-soul entity in a human body. If you want to grow and make progress, the time for belittling or 'putting yourself down' is over. Your "I AM" God Presence is not floating around somewhere in space out of your body. The fact is that your True Self has never left or abandoned you for even a moment. The reason I choose not to use the word 'Higher Self' in this book is because it implies that there is a 'Lower Self', which we usually judge. This word usage creates an illusion of duality, and it is exactly this illusion that we focus on transmuting and healing within our consciousness.

I prefer to use the words 'True Self', 'Real Self' or 'I AM God Presence' (refer to Self-Help Manual, page 118). This affirms our own transcendent intelligence which is an aspect of the all encompassing, universal consciousness of God. Human 'person-ality' is that part of you that receives, assimilates and reflects back the data from all the stimuli you receive from parents, friends, lovers, and your universal "I AM" Presence. How you respond and what you do with that data or information-energy-vibration, is what makes up your personal identity. This is a result and experience of many lifetimes of impressions and cellular memories of how you handled and interacted with various life's challenges. One of these challenges is to learn love and acceptance for the human aspect of oneself – to learn compassion, gentleness and understanding for our frail human feelings, to learn to honor all that is human and vulnerable within us. **By ignoring or rejecting basic human emotions, we are once more cutting off a part of our vital, sustaining life force which in turn can endanger our health.**

THE SEVEN STEP RECOVERY PROGRAM
**Step 1: Acknowledge the emotion,** whether it is anger, jealousy, envy, fear, hurt, frustration, etc. Allow yourself to fully feel and experience that emotion. Give yourself permission to fully express that feeling in depth, so you are not denying the spontaneous release of that emotion. As you release your emotional expression, you may want to direct it into a pillow, or another inanimate object. Do not project or direct it at any person or animal. Do not direct it at yourself. I suggest going outside into nature, where you can have some privacy and space. After you express your emotional release, go over to a tree and hug it to ground your energy back into the earth.

**Step 2: Don't judge yourself or the emotion** that you're experiencing as right or wrong, good or bad, high or low. Simply acknowledge its existence by accepting all that you are experiencing as valid.

**Step 3: Validate yourself** for expressing your emotions freely and by recognizing them. Give yourself credit for having the courage to face and express these emotions.

**Step 4: Re-parenting: Nurturing and Mothering Your Inner Child**   Give yourself some time to move into a quiet place where you can center yourself. Start the guided light meditation attunement (see page 40) and call on your "I AM" Presence: Beloved Holy Spirit "I AM" in my being, I open myself to a total healing of the cause, effect record . . . (See page 40-41)

**Step 5: Forgiveness**
As you and your inner child become one in that soft golden-white light, begin to slowly shift your focus into your heart center. Visualize a soft fragrant white-golden rose with soft pink on the edges inside your heart. Feel its soothing fragrance and soft, loving presence. Slowly bring your attention to the very center bud of the rose and visualize a soft, pink light emanating from this center. Slowly breathe in the essence of that soft, pink light, and as you exhale, visualize that same soft, pink light spreading its radiance throughout your body and creating a fountain of sparkling white, golden and pink light that cascades all around you. As you continue this breathing exercise and visualization (for at least 5-15 minutes), bring your attention back into the center of the rose in your heart. Now visualize a tiny infant inside the center of your heart-rose. That infant is your inner child, the new inner self that you are birthing. As you breathe, you

become one with this inner child and it becomes one with you. You are joined together within your heart in one loving embrace, in One heartbeat. Ask your inner child for forgiveness as it pours out unconditional love for you. Ask that all people, including yourself, that are involved in the cause of your emotional pain (including your own birth, the parents, lovers, relatives, friends, work colleagues etc.) are completely forgiven for any abuse they may have caused you. Now pick a person with whom you are currently having major challenges with. Visualize this person standing (people, or your adult self) in front of you, as you begin to breathe out that same essence of white, golden-pink light from the heart of your inner child. Begin to surround that person with the same color, light and fragrance as you have visualized surrounding yourself during your breathing attunement. During this process of forgiveness, you are also releasing yourself from the self-judgment, guilt and pain that you have identified with for so long. Not only are you releasing the limiting thought forms about the other person, but you are also releasing your own emotional body from further constriction. This brings great peace and comfort to your whole body. Keep breathing the white, golden-pink colors of forgiveness in and out until you feel completely at ease with yourself and the other person. **Realize that what's important is NOT waiting for the other person to change, but for you to release yourself from a pattern of abuse and powerlessness to a state of empowerment and peace.**

## Step 6: Transmutation
Transmutation is a process that dissolves 'old' limiting concepts, patterns of belief that have limited our awareness of self and transforms it into higher octaves of divine

perfection. As the process of dissolving is initiated, there is a re-structuring of atomic sub-particles (thoughts carry energy) that are in harmony with universal vibrations of perfection. An original state of Grace is re-established during this process of transmutation, much like the ancient alchemists who were able to convert base metals into gold. The old, denser crystallized thought forms and beliefs, those that have been the cause of so much pain and suffering, are literally dissolving as a re-structuring of the original cellular blueprint takes place to produce a state of health through affirming vibrations and thought forms of wholeness and perfection.

The color violet is the color of transmutation and acceleration. Since violet is the fastest vibrating color in the light spectrum, it has the greatest power and capacity to dissolve denser energies and vibrations by raising the atomic structure to a higher frequency of light. When you feel that both yourself and the other person have been sufficiently saturated in the white, golden, pink rose light, begin the following visualization: The person standing in front of you moves closer to you, extending their open arms and hands open to embrace you. As you extend your arms to embrace this person, you begin to feel a powerful vibration of ultra-violet light energy moving up through the earth where you stand. Visualize this violet light as a powerful, electronic spiral surrounding you both as you are joined together. As you feel the spiralling violet light enfolding you, the violet light begins to spiral into deeper tones of violet; it then continues spiralling around you both into a cone shape all the way around your heads and above your heads. This vibrating spiral of violet light increases in magnitude as you both accept more love to flow between you. Both energy fields are being completely transmuted into

ONE great frequency of light, harmony and perfection. As soon as the spiral reaches the crown chakra, it immediately starts spiralling back down into the earth and then as it spirals upward again, it enfolds you both in a pyramid, cone shape of the most dazzling, brilliant violet light. You can also do this meditation–visualization with any person with whom you wish to have a clearing. This can also be done between your 'inner child' and your 'adult self'. It is a very effective process in clearing old, stuck patterns from within your subconscious and etheric body. (More information on this violet light ray and its use can be found on page 147 in the Self-Help Manual).

**Step 7: Acceptance and Integration**
As the above steps are completed, begin to acknowledge your healing by affirming and giving thanks to your I AM God Presence for assisting you during this process of release, transmutation and healing. As you bring your consciousness back into the room you are in (after the violet spiral visualization), gather all the positive healing light energy around you and draw it back into yourself. As you do so, visualize a pure emerald green healing light surrounding you. Emerald green is the cosmic color for healing. As this green healing light radiates around and saturates your aura, feel the rejuvenation of all your cells; breathe this green light into your lungs, your heart, your organs, and into your emotional body (solar plexus) by placing the palms of your hands on your abdomen. Affirm silently or aloud: "In the name of my God Presence, I AM affirming and accepting my total healing in all areas of my being . . . in my etheric body . . . in my mental body . . . in my emotional body . . . and in my physical body. I now accept the wholeness in which I was created to fully manifest in all parts of myself. I AM THE HEALING PRESENCE AND POWER OF GOD'S INFINITE LOVE AND

LIGHT MANIFEST IN EVERY ATOM, CELL, ORGAN, AND TISSUE OF MY PHYSICAL BODY. For a few minutes, repeat this affirmation several times, and **allow** the soothing green healing light to continue permeating your entire being with its essence. You will definitely notice a soothing and healing balm surrounding and relaxing your entire solar plexus area, restoring harmony, balance and peace in your whole body. As the palms of your hands are on your solar plexus, visualize a concentration of deep emerald light radiating from your heart into and through your hands into your solar plexus. When you feel ready, slowly come back from your meditation and slowly stretch your whole body until you feel integrated into your physical body. These currents of energy and vibration are physically manifesting and entering your body, restructuring cellular memories, transmuting, dissolving and raising the atomic structure of your entire physical body. What a great service you are rendering yourself and planet earth! Acknowledge yourself for regaining your own power and strength. Accept how wonderful it is that you have the power within you to make these major shifts at any time that it is necessary.

I recommend playing the recording *ANGEL LOVE* (See Appendix) during this entire meditation. This music will accelerate your healing process as well as your creative visualizations.

# PART III

# RECLAIMING
# YOUR TRUE IDENTITY
# AND
# CREATING LOVING
# RELATIONSHIPS

IN THE QUIET ALTAR OF MY HEART

MY MIND LOOKS IN

TO LEARN A NEW LANGUAGE

OF THE SOUL

# 11

# RECLAIMING YOUR TRUE IDENTITY

How we feel about ourselves and how we see ourselves in relation to the world and culture around us creates a patterning for our personal identity. This includes our belief systems, perceptions, judgments, and of course the influence of our parents and our early childhood development. There are two basic types of identity patterning:

1. THE OUTER SOCIAL–ENVIRONMENTAL IDENTITY includes influences of environment, society and early childhood development, conditioned by parents, social beliefs, role-playing, performance-oriented, competitive, sees material structure of world as reality.

2. THE INNER SOUL SEEKER IDENTITY breaks away from stereotype role-playing, tradition, limited belief systems, questions the validity of present social systems and structures, seeks new, more functional and emotionally fulfilling levels of communication, seeks within to find own inner truth.

### THE OUTER SOCIAL-ENVIRONMENTAL IDENTITY

The first and most common form of social identity starts to form in the womb. To take this a few steps further, we can go back to the moment of conception and look at what both the mother and father were feeling at the time they made love. To go back even further, we can be aware of past-life influences that created the present psychological and emotional pattern of the infant. All these influences play a vital role in shaping the present emotional, psychological, and personal state of each being that incarnates on earth. This includes the concepts, fears, and belief patterns of our parents and the kind of emotional reinforcement and validation we received as children. Naturally this crosses over into our social interaction with others and how we relate to the world outside our immediate family. How we fit into various social roles such as our educational system from kindergarten up through our university training, how we relate to the social structures and institutions around us, become an important patterning for our social identity during these crucial years of our human development.

### THE INNER SOUL-SEEKER IDENTITY

This second type of identity pattern is much less common and represents more the spiritual seekers, those of us who are not satisfied with surface information, who want to probe deeper into the hidden, more subtle realms of consciousness. **They want to find the missing link between their own personal power and identity and how to relate to the outside world, without compromising their integrity and self-worth.**

This part of the human population are the soul-searchers who are not satisfied with the present social belief systems, the values and principles of economic–military establishments, and a competitive lifestyle. Instead, they look deeper within themselves to find their own personal meaning of truth and Reality. From this experiential development and awareness, they create their own foundation and value system whether it is in harmony with society's standards and beliefs or not. This does not mean a rejection of society, social standards, or judgment of another being's personal choice of reality. It simply means that within the process of introspection and diving into one's very inner core of being, certain belief patterns that were unconsciously accepted as true and real, start to dissolve as a new, more fullfiling and functional meaning of LIFE replaces the old, dysfunctional patterns of abuse.

To get in touch with one's own personal emotional and psychological state of being, takes some distancing from the distractions of outer stimuli and the world around us. It takes stepping off the treadmill of self-imposed distractions that we unconsciously create in order not to face our pain. It takes strength and courage to break free from these addictive role-patterns that our current social values unconsciously support. It is however, the first vital step to recovering and re-claiming a healthy, emotionally fulfilling, personal identity that is completely free from self-abuse and addiction.

# 12

# THE HEALING AND TRANSFORMATION
# OF MY HUMAN IDENTITY

Like most of us, I started this life as a 'victim'. It took over thirty five years of living in a 'victim's' emotional, mental and physical body for me to experience the cruelty, brutality, violence, terror and fear of a world to which I felt no relationship. During these years, I 'played out' the reactive behavior patterns of a victim, and didn't feel totally present in my physical body since a part of me didn't really want to be here anyway. It was a great struggle just to maintain my emotional - mental balance and feel good about being here on the earth. As a 'victim', I unconsciously chose many experiences of self-abuse that created emotional and physical pain and resistance to the world around me as well as in close intimate relationships. During the six major, intimate relationships that I have experienced, a recurring pattern of emotional and sexual abuse was unconsciously re-enacted, since I did not understand or have any awareness of its cause. All I thought was: "Here I am, being loving and kind, and sharing my deeper Self, and I'm constantly getting treated as a doormat." Some of the most recurring emotional patterns of abuse were painful feelings of great rejection and abandonment. These patterns played themselves out to such a dramatic degree that my whole inner foundation was shaken as my ego-identity started to crumble and dissolve. As my old, hurt Self and VICTIM, "poor me, how could this be happening to me" started to resurface, I began to experience several major stages of death and dying. It was at this point that the whole inner foundation of my personal human development began moving through a major transformation and awakening which has allowed me to write this book and to share some of these personal experiences with you.

My inner awakening started when I RECOGNIZED and admitted to myself that I was the creator of these painful experiences, and **that I was really creating self-abuse by allowing myself and others to relate on this dysfunctional level, without being consciously aware of it. I felt like I was the one that was being abused by someone else. It felt like someone was always doing this to me, and I didn't understand why.** Does that sound like a familiar scenario in your own life? I experienced deep states of depression and grief after the termination of each of these relationships. I felt so much injustice and anger towards my lovers. The pain was lodged so deeply that I almost became numb to it. I would create meaningful distractions like starting a new painting or a new piece of music that would express my longing and unfulfilled desire for healing and wholeness. I think that this is why some of my music has been so transforming and healing to others. Each album represents a 'breakthrough' and new level of healing within myself. Everything I didn't get in a relationship, I would make sure was created through the music. The music and its creation became my surrogate lover, a marriage that would last forever. All the confirmation and acknowledgment I wanted from a lover, I started learning how to give to myself from my inner being through the music. This was still a very lonely place for me to be as I could really share this inner part of my Self with only a few people.

These challenging, dysfunctional relationships and experiences actually motivated me to reach into a much deeper part of my inner being. There, I discovered the spiritual value and meaning of a new aspect of myself that I had never touched before. I was forced to look at my present values and assess what part of life had the greatest and deepest meaning to me. Did this mean being able to fit into a mold or social structure where I felt no connection in order to be 'normal' and acceptable by others? A major breakthrough occured when I realized that there is no such thing as 'normal'. Every single human being on this earth is unique and has his or her own value system, feelings, thoughts, and vibrations. Each person has an emotional and spiritual path that is totally individual and unique in its personal expression and is different from any other human being. Deep inside each being is a Presence that stands free from the judgments of the world. There is a place where true self-love lives, a place were only the deepest personal feelings matter. YES, A PLACE WHERE FEELINGS REALLY MATTER!

I remember coming into this incarnation with a first thought and reaction: "SHOCK! THE EARTH PLANE IS A TRAP AND I FEEL TRAPPED IN THIS BODY. IT IS A SHOCK TO BE HERE, AND IT'S CHOKING ME. THERE IS NO LOVE HERE." This was the birth of a 'classic victim' to the core. Born in West Germany in the 1950's, I remember as a little boy looking through tall barbed-wire fences and seeing soldiers in uniforms carrying blood-stained bodies on stretchers and hearing air-raid sirens screaming loudly.

I remember asking my mother why were they doing this, and what did it mean. She answered that they were just routine, 'make-believe' maneuvers, and everything was fake, even the blood was made from ketchup. The memory of this scene was deeply imprinted in my mind. I never understood why people and animals had to endure such violence and suffering. However, my own personal suffering and violence was of another nature.

As I mentioned earlier in the book, **all souls who incarnate on earth, come here to heal some form or aspect of self-abuse. Otherwise, there would be no purpose for us to be in such an abusive and challenging environment.** The earth plane teaches us self-mastery. We learn how to release and heal our own human creation of suffering and pain. Many souls that have incarnated from higher dimensions still have to learn certain lessons about the abuse of personal power, about loving, and about how to direct their intelligence so it is in alignment with Divine Will. Learning how to share with our brothers and sisters, learning how to give and receive, learning how to be vulnerable, and learning how to trust again are the lessons and challenges many of us face in our daily life here on earth.

WHAT IS THIS INTIMACY THAT WE ALL SO LONG TO HAVE IN OUR LIVES? Is it acceptance and acknowledgment of all parts of ourselves from another person we love? Is it exposing all our fears and desires without expecting love in return? **Or is it exposing and opening up a part of ourselves that we have no control over?** I think this last question touches a vital nerve in all of us. **Can you learn to trust yourself enough to be able to surrender to love, without losing your own personal power or will?** This seems to be life's greatest challenge. It is through the act of surrendering and letting go, that we open our own 'Pandora's box' to expose and release the many hidden layers of our fear, shame, guilt, judgment, self-doubt, and self-denial.

My personal suffering was my identification and personalization of 'my own pain' and the whole spectrum of abuse that the human experience relives over and over until we are at a breaking point with our emotional and mental patterns. Somewhere during early childhood development, I temporarily lost my true spiritual identity and became involved in the causes and effects of human experiences that I had no control over because somewhere long ago, I had crystallized the belief that being in the physical body was not spiritual, and there was no love here on earth. Oh yes, I knew of love somewhere. I was used to love and being loved on such a deep level in a dimension where there was only pure Love and Light and Harmony before I incarnated on the earth plane. So for me to experience what most human beings experience on the earth plane as 'love' was a distortion and a primitive approximation of a love I knew that had no boundaries or limits.

My greatest challenge was adjusting to this denser vibration of love energy on the earth. I became afraid and mistrustful of anything physical (represented by the first two chakras, survival and sexuality). I witnessed traumatic emotional abuse and cruelty in the world around me. Arguments, quarrels, seeing how people treated one another, became an intolerable reality to my inner child. This child could not accept such a distorted portrayal of love. For about twenty five years, as a result, I was in complete denial of the physical part of myself because of the abuse that I associated with those areas (first chakra-survival, fear of physical reality and second chakra-pro-creation reality). This dysfunctional state became a cata-lyst for the healing of my human self. As I started to rediscover and reconnect with my inner child by giving it all the love, acknowledgment, nurturing and support it needed, I started to repattern and replace the self-abusive emotional patterns with new, loving programs of self-love, and acceptance of the physical plane through lov-ing, healing affirmations. (See Self-Help Manual, page 124 ). Gradually I started to feel safe in this physical di-mension, and realized that I had special gifts to bring to this plane of Reality, as I visualized the physical plane loving and supporting me for who I am. These affirma-tions, together with meditation and inner work greatly assisted me in embracing all my desires, needs and feel-ings in unconditional love. I learned to give to myself the love that I so much craved from others.

## STABILIZING MY NEW IDENTITY

All levels of human growth involve communication and relationship. What is your relationship to your human body? How do we relate to being in a male or female body? How do we relate or express what we feel to others? What is our frame of reference when we relate to our own growth and the world around us? Are we locked into archetypal role models to give us our identity? What makes you who you are? EVERYTHING IN LIFE IS ALWAYS IN MOTION AND IN MUTABLE RELATIONSHIP TO THE WHOLE. **Our evolving pattern and perception of Self and per-sonal identity comes from our understanding of what WHOLE really IS, and our relationship to that WHOLENESS.** Each being will define Whole or Wholeness in a different way, depending on their own personal childhood devel-opment. Whole can mean complete and healthy. It can mean a little village, or tribe, a nation, a planet, global consciousness or the universe. In some cultures the concept of wholeness is confined to their own little village, tribe and territory. Some have a more expanded cosmology, like the Hopi Indians whose concept of the Whole relates to the very foundation and flow of their own lives in harmony and relationship to nature and universal cycles of creation. Each culture and religion has their own cosmology and concept of the 'whole' and what this means. Unfortunately in our present contemporary culture and civilization, wholeness is viewed mainly as becoming independent, successful, and acquiring more material wealth and status with little or no regard to the environment or how our actions affect the rest of life and this planet.

**There is a great need for education and communication regarding the inherent balance and sustenance of nature and how to work in harmony with her in order to achieve our own wholeness and balance.** AS WE LEARN HOW TO BRING MORE HARMONY AND BALANCE INTO OUR OWN BODIES AND MINDS, WE BEGIN THE PERSONAL NURTURING PROCESS THAT IN TURN ENHANCES OUR RELATIONSHIP WITH ALL OF NATURE AND THE LIFE AROUND US. THIS HELPS US TO BECOME MORE CONSCIOUS OF LIFE ITSELF, AS WE LEARN GREATER LOVE, RESPECT AND APPRECIATION FOR THE GIFT OF LIFE.

Another big challenge for me earlier in life was that I did NOT RELATE to the world around me. I simply did not have any relationship to what I saw around me, especially in large cities. I felt very "cut off" from modern civilization which during that time, I perceived as primitive, cruel and dead to life itself. I couldn't understand why people didn't reach out to one another and express more love. Everyone looked the other way when passing one another on the street with no acknowledgment of the other person's existence. In buses and subways, people would bury their faces in books or newspapers so they wouldn't have to look at one another. To me this was death. It was exactly this fear of love and life that I saw in others that helped me in my own Inner Awakening. Many times negativity is a catalyst to motivate or propel us into the next level of our growth and development.

I have asked the universe countless times, "God, if you are such a loving, compassionate Being, how can you ALLOW such widespread abuse of power and greed to corrupt so many innocent people on earth?" I couldn't understand how we in the twentieth century could allow such abuse of human life by allowing 40,000 children to die of starvation daily, while spending billions of dollars on arsenals and the Star Wars project, defense, and chemical warfare (including preservatives in food) that intentionally shortens the life span of a human being. Looking at these dysfunctional global socio-economic political systems in retrospect, I became aware that perhaps there IS a cosmic purpose or divine reason why such abuse is allowed on this planet. I probed deeper and deeper for an answer, until I started to realize that **part of our present cycle of planetary evolution (Pluto in Scorpio, Death and Regeneration) involves a major release and transmutation of Self-Abuse and Death.**

Many levels of Self-Abuse are unconsciously 'projected' collectively on the environment, social institutions, and various other life forms including humans beings. **The quality of life on our planet has become so critically low and abusive that it literally propels each one of us to look inward toward SPIRIT and to find the**

**solutions within.** As the polarization continues to increase on our planet, all negativity becomes more pronounced so it can serve as a catalyst for great inner growth and awakening. Each one of us begins to learn how to create our own stable foundation and identity that is not affected by the turmoil and negative illusions of the 'outer world'. To master this process you actually learn to become a 'superman'. No man is an island unto himself. We are all affected by every living creature on earth in one way or another. How we choose to relate to this phenomena of life is what creates the pattern of our social persona or outer identity. We can become strong, and still be open and vulnerable. Or we can continue playing out our 'victim' dramas and perpetuate self-abuse. **We will always magnetize abusers to us, when we are still in the 'victim' mode.**

Continuing this process of introspection and probing within for more answers, I gradually started to formulate within my sphere of relationships an awareness by **learning to discern between the projected creation of Illusion (Human Mind) and Reality (True Self). This does not mean that discernment is judgment, but rather a "weeding-out" process that allows us to make healthier choices in life;- ones that support and nurture our well-being.** I repeatedly asked myself the question: "DOES THIS CHOICE REALLY SUPPORT THE HIGHEST TRUTH FOR MY GROWTH AND DEVELOPMENT?" I know that I have always related to the essence of love, light, harmony, intelligence, truth, and peace. I naturally relate easier to expansion rather than contraction. It's more natural for me. So I began my own personal journey of developing more positive, loving human relationships that would assist me in stabilizing my own nurturing identity of healing, self-empowerment, and creativity. This became the focus of my personal growth as I started to make more conscious choices of the kind of people and energy I wanted around me; those that would support my new identity and integrity without compromise. Creating this new stable foundation for a healthier Self is necessary in order to be in balance and harmony with life, nature, and the universe. This includes our relationship to spirit, the earth, other beings, and other intelligent life forms in the universe.

As I began to stabilize my priorities and anchor them into my practical, daily life, I started to attract a new level of relationships that were more balanced and fulfilling. These new relationships became a mutual system of support, integrity, and creative communication resulting in an expansion of awareness and understanding that was very healing and beneficial to all of us. **Refining this level of communication between ourselves and others is an on-going process as we become clearer and more focused in our awareness of love and its expanding intelligence and sensitivity within us and all life.**

This expanded level of relationship and communication also exposed all those parts of my human identity that were not loved, embraced, or accepted during my childhood. These revelations became more vivid as the loud cry of my inner child increased and more human issues that needed love, acceptance, embrace and freedom reappeared. One of these issues was **my need to be touched and held more, to express my sexuality without inhibition, to feel safe with someone on a one-to-one level**. I needed to learn to live peacefully with these desires and to be okay with these basic, unfulfilled needs for love and nurturing. I had to face any fears of intimacy that lingered subconsciously in my emotional, mental, and physical body, as I was so terrified of being rejected and abandoned.

Another issue was the feeling that I somehow didn't really belong here on earth. I felt so separate and alone most of the time. I had to face these fears of being alone with myself for so many years. I learned how to bond with my inner Self and to release the many cords and attachments to people and relationships that were no longer a part of my life. During this period I developed a great reserve of loving inner strength and endurance. I think the great shock and trauma I experienced at birth contributed greatly to my separation and grief. I felt so severed from the interdimensional light realms from where I came. **The contrast of dimensions was so pronounced that my greatest challenge was to lovingly embrace the vibrational density here on earth without judging it.**

I began to realize that because I judged the earth as a "lower" planet, I would re-create this feeling in all my human relationships in the world around me. My human projection of this "lower density" would mirror itself back to me, especially in close, intimate situations. **My worldly experiences simply reflected back to me my own inner judgment of earthly life.** The feeling of conflict and separation inside was at times truly unbearable and deeply painful. **When at last, I became aware that something in my own belief system was creating these feelings of separation, pain, suffering, sacrifice, and grief and NOT THE WORLD OUT THERE,** I was truly on the verge and wings of my first significant breakthrough toward reclaiming my true identity.

**One of the most difficult challenges I had to face was the recognition that I myself was responsible for creating everything that was happening to me. As a direct result of my own judgments, fears, feelings and beliefs, I was determining a pattern of reality that reflected back to me those very feelings, thoughts and beliefs.** When the pain and grief became too intense to bear, I decided that I must take charge of my own life. It was at this point that my own personal power began birthing itself. My first question was, "Why did I create this distortion of love in my life? When did this form of self-abuse begin?" **Taking charge of my life involved taking full responsibility for everything that I experience in life as a CONSCIOUS PERSONAL CHOICE.** My old patterns started to shift dramatically with this revelation. When I became aware of the fact that I had a CONSCIOUS CHOICE to alter my reality, I started to focus on spiritual tools and teachings that would help me **to reclaim my true power and identity.**

This inspiration led me on a spiritual pilgrimage to India in 1976, where I studied various forms of meditation and spiritual practices. These were very helpful, but I still retained an image and need of a 'guru-worship' or an ideal, archetypal, nurturing father-figure in order to fulfill certain aspects of my emotional needs. Part of me was still looking 'outside of myself' for the answers.

When I returned to the United States in 1977, I experienced another major breakthrough. Within two weeks of my return, I was given a pamphlet on "THE VIOLET FLAME" by St. Germain. As I had come back from India with most of my wardrobe in violet, and had visions of violet light during my meditations, I was instantly attracted to this literature. Within two weeks I was on my way to Mt.

Shasta in northern California where some of the first teachings of St. Germain manifested in the early 1930's through the mystical experiences of Guy Ballard. He was taken inside this sacred mountain by St. Germain. This place magnetized and fascinated me. I had the feeling that here was an interdimensional, mystical space. AND IT IS!

The Ascended Master teachings that I studied in Mt. Shasta focus on personal self-empowerment and self-mastery and this attracted me very much. The focus is directed toward learning self-mastery by honoring your own Inner "I AM God Presence". **The teaching is not to give your personal power away to external 'projections' of divinity, but in becoming one with your own inner I AM GOD PRESENCE.** I learned that every thought, every spoken word, every action and feeling carries a vibration of energy that radiates into the universe and has an immediate effect on our mental, emotional, physical and etheric bodies as well as upon the rest of the world. I started to become more aware of my emotions and thought patterns and how what I was thinking and saying had an effect on my own state of well-being. During a period of approximately ten years in Mt. Shasta, I focused intensely on spiritual healing affirmations and meditations. They have deeply transformed my life and my awareness of Self. Many of these affirmations appear in the Self Help Manual of this book (See page 124) and on the Guided Meditation cassette: *LIVING IN YOUR HEART* (See Appendix).

As I set out to re-pattern my new identity with these healing affirmations daily, together with creative visualizations, my inner Self began adopting this new way

**of seeing, accepting and being.** I WAS GRADUALLY BIRTH-
ING MY TRUE SELF. As I let go of 'victim' consciousness and
made the conscious choice to heal all forms and causes of
self-abuse, a whole new world of support, love and possibilities began opening up for me. **I felt more in charge of
my life as I acknowledged not only my new spiritual
identity, but also lovingly acknowledged all of my
human feelings, desires, and needs without judging
them as right or wrong.** This process lifted me into a
whole new world of the acceptance of my human-ness. I
felt better about myself as I learned to recognize and
embrace my emotional needs and desires without self-
condemnation.

This shift in consciousness cleared a new space for me
to enfold all my human-ness in the nurturing embrace of
unconditional love and self-acceptance. It became easier
not to identify exclusively with my own personal emotional needs and desires. During this time I learned great
compassion for the suffering that we as human beings
live through in order to master the illusions of our own
human creation. If I did not 'fit in' into someone else's
standards of acceptable behavior, it provided only greater
impetus to love and accept those very parts of myself
more. Sometimes we have 'to stand alone' in order to find
our own path of Light. The more deeply we are connected
to our TRUE SELF, the less we depend on 'public opinion'
or the superficial role models of society. When I realized
just how much abuse existed in the social media, especially in the motion picture, television and music industries, it amplified my strength and will to create music
and art that was of a healing nature; music that would
uplift the awareness and consciousness of humanity to a
greater level of love and intelligence.

WHAT BECAME REALITY FOR ME, AND WHAT DID I SEE AS ILLUSION? I saw illusion as the many 'fragments' of the human persona scattered about on a planet separated from its Source, disconnected from Life and Nature, disconnected from its Own True Self. I saw the phenomena of birth and death as an illusion, as well as pleasure and pain and the entire, conditioned state of duality within our minds and consciousness as illusion. I saw compromises, lies, abuse of power and competition, as a way to get ahead in the world, as forms of illusion. I also saw that the cause of all human suffering is ignorance and the lack of will to know the Truth of Life and Creation, and therefore to know oneself. I saw that when we 'stop running away' from ourselves, we can heal the illusion of duality within our own thoughts and beliefs. **Literally everything was an illusion except LOVE and TRUTH. I realized that the pursuit of love and truth was the only Reality that we 'take with us' when we depart from this physical earth dimension. Nothing else is real and remains with us. Only the moments of love, of giving and sharing, of aspiring towards illumined Truth, Love, and Intelligence remain and become our passport into the next phase of our evolutionary development.** Out of this realization a new beauty, wisdom, and meaning was born that would guide me into a fuller realization of these two universal qualities. There are times when I have no sense of Self and times when I feel I am everyone and at the same time no one.

# 13

# THE QUANTUM SHIFT:
# THE BIRTHING OF MY TRUE SELF

During the creative transmission of my music and its manifestation into form, my personal identity becomes transparent allowing the Ascended Masters and other beautiful interdimensional beings of light to co-create and transmit refined, celestial frequencies of sound, light and intelligence through me. This has also greatly expanded my awareness and identity. In 1986 in Germany, I had a profound experience that changed my life. I was just recovering from an abusive relationship that was very challenging, as it brought up so much of my own pain and showed me parts of myself that I was still not totally accepting.

The spiritual experience that profoundly changed my life the most so far, happened one evening in Munich where I played a private concert for three close friends in a small healing center. At one point during the concert, I saw a ball of light on the ceiling. As I started to tune into that light, the four of us went on a cosmic journey for over thirteen hours. We all entered a heightened state of awareness as we expanded together into a dimension of light that is beyond description. Very difficult to put into words, it was a pure state of Grace that blessed us very deeply by revealing to us the many levels and layers of our soul and spiritual identity. During this major initiation, I was blessed with the meeting and reunion with my Essence-Twin (See Self-Help Manual, Mother of Pearl Ray page 177-182) who is my other half and lives in an ascended light body  and serves the earth's evolution as well as other dimensions of light. This RE-UNION transformed my every perception of relationships and identity to a whole new and expanded level of consciousness. All my concepts of Self began dissolving, as I was experiencing my new Birth into Wholeness, One-Ness and complete Empowerment. There was no greater love in the whole universe than to reunite with this part of my Soul-Essence. I knew that this is what I was really searching for in all my intimate relationships. This level of profound, irreplaceable INTIMACY gave me the love, the power, the strength, the support and acceptance, the clarity, wholeness and fulfillment that I had always longed for  but never consicously experienced before, especially on the earth plane.

Since this profound initiation, I have never been the same person and have grown immeasurably as a result. I have learned to assimilate more, and to 'let go of' more than I ever thought was possible.  A completely new value system emerged in relationship to myself. It helped me tremendously in healing any 'left-over' patterns of self-abuse.  I was 'a newly transformed and integrated, whole Being, with my Essence Twin always One with me on all levels of Being, always present within my Self as Myself.  At the same time, on another level, the challenge became even greater, as the responsibility to maintain and sustain this clear state of Being in this physical dimension became increasingly more difficult. The contrast between the external world of form and my new Identity became more pronounced. Part of my human self was really struggling to accept and integrate this new sense of wholeness. Somewhere deep within my human experience, a tiny part of me still clung to the illusion that I wasn't worthy of such love and inner power.

At this point, however, there just was no turning back. A choice to accept or reject this new Self was not even a consideration. Deep down inside I always knew and felt the reality of a powerful Inner Presence of Light. I just didn't understand my personal connection and relationship to that Presence. This 'new' Self was learning how to relate on a transpersonal level with all parts of Itself within a world of form as well as within the inner dimensions of consciousness in order to access new levels of intelligent communication and transmission, as they are channelled through into the earth plane.

As loving acceptance and appreciation of my true Self deepens, I realize that I AM the full embodiment of this re-unified Self. I feel so empowered when I affirm this truth, and remember who I really AM. The beauty and inspiration of this new Self is that at times any sense of 'personal identity' is totally dissolved. This is a process that involves adjusting, adapting, and moving with the present flow of energy as it is manifesting. This heightened state of awareness also challenges my relationship to the physical plane as it teaches me greater trust and surrender. Since the universe and I are One, I am learning to trust more in myself and allow any limiting concepts of self-denial to simply fall away. It takes courage to relate to others from this transpersonal space because many people may not understand the loving intention behind this form of communication. They may personalize and internalize the experience, many times resulting in misunderstanding. In such cases, communication needs to be openly clarified or put into a language that is relevant and one that the other person can easily understand.

Another focus of this 'new' identity was becoming fully conscious and aware of my ability to love myself for who I am, without the need to get approval or acceptance from others and the external world. **This includes the loving acceptance of all aspects of my human self as well as my I AM God Presence. Once this love and self respect flowers, I then have the freedom to love and embrace all life around me as part of my own self and the universe. This freedom graces me with the love, acceptance and trust required to manifest whatever I need in my life.**

One day while driving my car in this small town of Mt. Shasta and looking all around at the people passing by, I realized then that I was just looking at different parts of myself. I visualized and projected a great wave of love and compassion toward all these people, whom I had considered as separate individuals so very different from myself, feeling no connection with them. This simple revelation altered my perception of relationships and the perspective of life around me. **When I treat others as I would like myself to be treated, it creates more harmony and love in all my interactions. This also expands my capacity to embrace and receive more love.**

# 14

# HEALING THE ILLUSION OF DUALITY:
## TRANSMUTING NEGATIVITY

I always had a difficult time dealing with negative energy or 'dark forces', for the most part because of my own judgments and fears, as I unconsciously externalized the projected 'split' in my consciousness, accepting and energizing it as reality. This dysfunctional belief, manifesting as the illusion of duality has also been the conditioned belief pattern of 'mass consciousness' on planet earth. **As I started to penetrate deeper into the cause and effect of human suffering, I became increasingly aware that HEALING THE ILLUSION OF DUALITY was really the greatest need challenging human growth and personal development during this time of our evolution.** The human mind has been conditioned into the belief that there is always an eternal struggle going on between light and dark, good and evil. **Remember, that whatever you focus on and energize, you bring into existence as your own living Reality. The real struggle of duality is the one that is within our own consciousness.** Unfortunately we externalize and project this duality into the world of form, and as a result, this affects many individuals in their daily interaction with one another. The human mind has been conditioned to act and react out of fear for survival and control. Our mind has been trained to judge, to analyze, to separate and compare, etc. We "buy into" the fear that there are 'dark forces', that sexuality is not spiritual, and that we really don't deserve love, happiness and fulfilling relationships on the earth all because of a belief in the illusion of duality.

**Healing our emotions and internal conflict regarding our relationship with the ONE, and our very own I AM PRESENCE is the focus of our true personal healing and the healing of the earth.** Once the illusion of duality is mastered here in "schoolroom" earth, a soul is ready to ascend to a more enlightened state of being and life form where there is no more need for conflict and suffering and, therefore, no existence or illusion of duality. This state can also be achieved here on the Earth NOW. There are presently many light workers on the planet who have consciously incarnated to facilitate this transformation of humanity and the healing of all life on this planet. Once we have mastered and accepted our oneness with the source of all life, God, Universal Intelligence, Love, call it what you will, and we have healed the illusion of duality within our own consciousness, there will be no more need for death and dying.

As we resist and stand in judgment of the projected 'negative polarity', we will continue to magnetize that undesireable energy into our lives. We need to reconcile that part of our self and say, **"I see you and accept you as a part of God. I embrace you in love, knowing that you come from the same Source as I, from One Universal Self. Thank you for giving me the opportunity to discern between the projected illusions of my mind and the Enlightened Reality of the One. I AM AT PEACE KNOWING that there is only ONE CREATOR, ONE INTEL-**

LIGENCE that surpasses and transcends all appearances and projected illusions of duality. This same POWER and PRESENCE is within me as it is within you. I lovingly make peace with my own inner God Presence, surrendering to its Higher Intelligence and Will, as it guides me into a clearer vision and truer Reality of my Self." When you begin to practice this powerful, transformational affirmation whenever you experience conflict or negativity within or around you, you will be amazed at how much quicker you will be able to release and transmute it. As you 'stand back', observe your inner process, and affirm the above to yourself, you will create and maintain greater peace and harmony in your life. As you align yourself with the ONE THAT LIVES WITHIN YOU, that ONE will reach out to you and support you as you heal any 'split' within your consciousness. REMEMBER: WHAT YOU ENERGIZE AND FOCUS ON IN YOUR HEART AND MIND IS WHAT YOU CREATE AS YOUR OWN REALITY. It is that simple! This is how the universe functions. It will test you over and over again until there is not a shadow of a doubt left within you that there is only ONE REALITY, and that is LOVE. The enemies in our life are only the projections of unhealed aspects of our own human creation. This can be judgments, fears, projections, guilt, and other forms of self-abuse. **Heal how you feel about yourself, and then ONLY LOVE REMAINS, and that is what and who we truly are.**

Just recently while editing the final 'mix' of my most recent musical album, *THE JOURNEY HOME: On Wings of Light*, (See Appendix) I was tested to the 'max' with major technical and computer problems. I worked in a very sophisticated high-tech sound studio with a professional, editing engineer. The computer would go 'on the blink' for several hours, and then 'jam after jam', test after test. My engineer expressed to me that he felt and sensed a power or presence of 'dark forces' trying to block this powerful transmission of light, since this album's energy has to do with the transmutation of 'the illusion of duality'. When my engineer voiced that "the 'dark forces' were trying to interfere", I replied that I will not accept that as my reality, even though I started to see myself as well, falling into the same old pattern and belief system by externalizing my present experience. This was a challenge for my artistic, technical and spiritual self. I decided to take some space and distance myself from this difficult situation, and said, **"God, if you really want to transmit this music and manifest it into physical form, please remove any and all obstacles and barriers within my own consciousness and beliefs that are creating these horrible clicks and pops on the computer." As difficult as it was, I had to look deeper within myself, probing for something still inside of me that would support the old fear and reaction by blaming my experience on someone or something outside of myself.** In response, I had to continuously shift and retune my consciousness in order to bring this album into its completion. (Just now as I am writing this page, the final editing process is taking place after a full nine months of intense, meticulous editing.) I had to look within and find whatever part of myself might still be holding on to the belief of 'someone having power over me', or 'some force that I could not control'.

These were all major issues in my life, and this album is perhaps one of the most powerful and magnificent musical transmissions that I have so far birthed into physical reality. It truly depicts the transmutation of human consciousness from a state of duality (darkness, conflict and ignorance) to that of One-ness and radiant Light. As I learned to embrace any resistance or negativity within my own belief system, thinking or feeling, I started 'seeing the light at the end of the tunnel'. Once I was able to recognize and accept that the reactive, projected illusions of duality were a result of my own thinking and belief system, the energy started to shift. As I made the committment to take full responsibility for the creation of all my experiences, the technical problems and "computor jams" started to disappear. At times, accepting this kind of responsibility is difficult without being overly critical and judgmental of yourself for your weaknesses and vulnerabilities. However, it's really a matter of learning more compassion for your inner child and giving yourself the gentle nurturing and validation that has been so suppressed or denied.

THE TWO BASIC PSYCHOLOGICAL FACTORS THAT CREATE AND REINFORCE SELF-ABUSE ARE: **SELF-JUDGMENT AND SELF-DENIAL.** This describes the healing process of human development. Ultimately, we cannot hold anything back from our true self. Loving self-honesty and compassion, without self-condemnation, creates a clear, vast and peaceful space for the ego to step aside and heal all dysfunctional patterns of abuse. Learning to BE HERE, FULLY PRESENT FOR YOUR INNER CHILD is probably the most healing gift you can give yourself. When your inner child feels safe, nurtured, validated, loved and accepted, you will experience a greater ease in expressing your feelings more spontaneously and intuitively. This opens up the door for your own beautiful, personal, creative expression to blossom. Your whole being rejoices and is at peace as you take the space and time to love, recognize, and honor who you really are.

# 15

## HEALING AND CREATING
## LOVING RELATIONSHIPS

One of the major lessons in our personal human development is learning how to create and maintain loving, supportive relationships with ourselves, other beings, and with all other life forms. What comes to mind in the word **relationship** is RELATIVITY, (as defined in Webster's dictionary): "The state of being dependent for existence or determined in nature, value, or some other quality by relation to something else". When we look at the definition of *relativity*, the first thought that comes to mind is 'a state of change', of mutability and flux, adapting and adjusting to the various aspects and interactions with other forms of life. There is also the aspect of interdependence and how each one of us is affected by other life forms around us. How we define our own boundaries and personal identity and how we develop our awareness in relation to the life around us, and the society in which we are part, determines the quality and depth of our interaction with others.

As our sense of Self starts to grow and develop, all the impressions we have received from our mother while in the womb have a profound effect on the psychological and personal development of the infant. The infant will absorb and take on the emotional imprints of the mother's experiences, i.e. her fears, worries, health concerns, as well as her joy, love, and nurturing aspects. If the mother is depressed a lot during her pregnancy, this also greatly affects the infant. The conflict and pain we experience from separation, abandonment, denial, rejection, and emotional projections by any parent or person raising us also greatly affects our emotional and personal development. Often, these abrasive emotional catalysts propel us to new levels of growth as we learn to develop healthier values of self-worth, self-love and self-acceptance. It also allows us to look deeper into our own emotional and physical needs, dependencies, and addictions. If the conflict and pain is not faced or healed, our subconscious mind will repeatedly program our emotions to react to this limiting, negative pattern. Until this pattern is consciously broken, we will continue to internalize our 'victim' role and carry with us the burden of a bitter attitude toward life.

Being able to take a magnifying lens and look into our recurring patterns of self-abuse in our intimate relationships, allows us to see the belief patterns we took on to shield and isolate ourselves from others, to protect ourselves from being hurt again. Our innermost human desire is to have love and intimacy, yet our conditioned emotional patterns recreate recurring, subconscious, 'sabotage' programs that shield us from the vulnerability and intensity of human intimacy. This is an unconscious, dysfunctional, mental–emotional pattern that causes us to create automatic defense barriers around ourselves that do not allow others into our own personal 'inner space' for fear of being rejected. In order to avoid becoming 'too close' to others, we create even greater ambition for more successful careers that will take up most of our time, or we drown ourselves in television, alcohol, drugs, sex, work-oholism, or other distractions in order not to face or expose our own vulnerability.

We protect ourselves from others by not showing certain parts of ourself. There are places within us that we wish others not to see. Usually this is an aspect of ourself that we have not accepted or one we do not feel good about. So we conveniently create multiple levels of distraction which turn into obsessive and addictive behavior patterns that keeps others at a 'safe' distance. We are afraid that if we show this side of ourselves, we will not be loved, and therefore rejected. Yet this very fear and avoidance creates a form of self-rejection that destroys any potential for a deep level of human intimacy. **Being able to see yourself as you are, in your exposed, vulnerable and defenseless state without judging and criticizing yourself, is to learn unconditional love and total self-acceptance**.

This is your key for healing all self-abuse and abusive patterns in all relationships. When you learn to be totally honest with yourself and your true feelings, by not hiding how you feel, you create a safety valve for others to feel more comfortable and open around you. This allows them the safe space to accept and express their own feelings without holding back. Anytime you hold something back, others automatically and instinctively feel this psychically and energetically, and the automatic reaction or response is to withdraw or pull away. This can be and usually is interpreted as **rejection**, by the person internalizing their feelings and not communicating or expressing them. On the other hand, the opposite can also be true. There are times when you are really honest and open with how you feel and others can be intimi-dated by your freedom and ease if their self-acceptance is not of an equally developed level. This phenomena cre-ates fear, judgment, rejection, and criticism that can be projected unto the person who is being open and sincere. However, in the long run, your honesty and self-accep-tance really helps the other person communicate with a part of himself or herself that is held in denial and even-tually will trigger some form of emotional and mental release. **Communication is the key for developing any form of relationship. Learning to communicate your feelings and thoughts with an open heart and an open mind will always facilitate the foundation for a loving relationship.**

Learning to trust all parts of yourself as you **get in touch with, feel, and express** anger, jealousy, frustration, lack, etc. without making yourself wrong, or blaming others for how you feel, is the first step toward acknowl-edging and accepting yourself in unconditional love. This develops greater compassion and understanding of your human nature, and accelerates the healing of your feelings and emotions. Learning to be REAL with all parts of yourself is the key to a healthy life and loving relationships. It's not that certain emotions are 'good' while others are 'bad'. The crucial point is **how we relate to** and express our own personal feelings and emotions without allowing them to sabotage our manifestation of love and fulfillment. If we are in denial or conflict with any of our emotions, we will attract conflict and denial from others that will mirror back to us those parts of ourselves we have not loved and accepted. Each being has his or her own personal challenge in this area. Life sets up these confrontational challenges as a catalyst for our growth and evolution. The challenge and conflict is in direct proportion and is relative to the level of self-healing and transformation that a person is capable of at a given time. No person on this earth is immune from this challenging process of inner growth. **We are all in this growing cycle together, and once we start to understand that each one of us faces our own degree or level of challenge, we can begin to dissolve our illusory 'projection' of an 'ideal' person that will fulfill all our needs.**

As we accept each other's human-ness by embracing both each other's strengths and weaknesses, a space of safety, trust, and freedom is created in which we are free to love one another unconditionally. This nurturing, unconditional love and acceptance creates the foundation for true intimacy in a relationship. **The challenge is not to try and 'reform' the other person to fit your own personal projection of perfection and an 'ideal', but to acknowledge the perfection and love that already exists, even if it is not always expressed or shown.** Every time you experience a conflict with another person, use that as an opportunity to love and acknowledge yourself more, without projecting a judgment on the other person or yourself. This is one of the most difficult things to do in any relationship. **Be aware that knowledge and human perception is limited to the relative nature of the mind, so it's wise to focus more on love and forgiveness, instead of 'getting stuck' with what we perceive or 'know' about each other.** This is a major key in developing loving, true friendships and intimate relationships.

DEFINING YOUR PERSONAL BOUNDARIES:
GETTING IN TOUCH
WITH YOUR EMOTIONAL NEEDS

I recently attended a men's workshop on healing sexual abuse. Almost every man present had a major issue of 'control' in relation to being violated. I learned much through observing and listening carefully to the personal testimonies and experiences of all the participants. Invariably, 95% of the men felt that they were somehow a 'victim' of some form of abuse, either mental, emotional, sexual, physical or a combination of the four. Naturally they had to set some defined boundaries in their relationships in order to establish a degree of emotional safety, setting up limits in order to protect themselves from the fear of further abuse. Learning to be receptive and sensitive to other people's emotional and psycho-sexual capacity and limits is an important factor in creating a foundation of trust and intimacy, as well as respect.

**As you heal your own issues of control and self-abuse, you will reach a point where you will know and feel that you can no longer be violated or abused by anybody.** This realization and self-acceptance releases you from all fear, as you complete the healing of even the tiniest issue within yourself that you have not loved or accepted. If there is still a small fragment of yourself that has not been fully loved, accepted and set free, it will manifest itself and be reflected back to you in a relationship. For example, you may have encountered a partner, lover, husband, wife, or parent shout at you out of control, "You're no good! You'll never amount to anything. Why don't you just give up?" As harsh and frightening as this may sound, the person who is expressing this rage, *may be* mirroring a part of yourself that you may not wish to look at or see. Do you have any feelings of not being good enough? Any doubts about your ability to achieve something truly meaningful in your life? Feelings like, "What's the use anyway? I should just give up." Even though these may be very small, subliminal and subconscious doubts that you are not even consciously aware of, a person close to you will probably **amplify** and **'act out'** this self-doubt until you become aware of your denial. We unconsciously recreate rejection over and over again until we have learned to accept and embrace all parts of ourselves, our shadows and fears, our pain, conflict, as well as the beautiful sunny places, rainbows, flowers, and butterflies. The raging storms we experience inside are the direct manifestation of our subconscious patterns of denial in the form of self-judgment, self-punishment, and the conflicting illusions/ projections of unhealed duality within our mind and perceptions. **What is harmful to human health is not so much the emotion itself, but the suppression and denial of our feelings and emotions, no matter how basic, raw, dense or refined they are.** If we focus on keeping our heart open, and our mind free from judgment, we are helping to facilitate our own healing as well as develop greater compassion for the suffering of all living beings.

### REDEFINING LOVE
### IN A HEALTHY RELATIONSHIP

At times we feel like we are "pushed into" a relationship, or we encounter a relationship with someone who really **"pushes our buttons"**. This could be a husband, wife, parent, sister, brother, or most likely a partner or lover. When you start to feel that your "buttons are being pushed" by someone, it is helpful to look at whether or not that person is actually treating you in a similar manner as your parents or a primary caretaker did during your childhood. This defensive reaction usually arises from an unhealed part of yourself that was wounded from some form of abuse either from a parent or a primary caretaker. When somebody "pushes your buttons", be a detective and know that this could be a clue for you to some part of your childhood that needs attention and healing. **Try to go back in time. If you are able to recognize a repetitive, consistent, emotional pattern of abuse that repeats itself in your intimate relationships, then you KNOW that you have a specific childhood pattern of abuse that needs healing and clearing.**

Our intimate partners or lovers will continue to play out this unconscious unhealed abuse, until we get in touch with the original pattern of abuse and are able to heal it. For example, there was a young woman who met an attractive man during a seminar. They both felt a very strong attraction and magnetism to one another. After the seminar was over, he promised her that he would get in touch with her within a week and they would get together. When after a week, he did not call or contact her, she was emotionally devastated, and did not understand why she had such a strong personal and emotional reaction to a situation with someone she hardly knew. When I started asking her about her father and how he treated her as a child and as an adult, she suddenly realized that he repeatedly promised her love and affection but never really expressed or manifested it. One day when he was in town lecturing at a university, he said he would call her and spend some special time with her, and take her out to dinner so the two could become closer. Again, the promises were made but never kept. So this psychological and emotional pattern of abuse manifested in all her intimate relationships with men, until she finally got in touch with the original pattern of abuse, and was able to forgive her father and set herself free to love again.

Many times as children, what we experienced as love, was not really love, but a dysfunctional pattern of attention. For example, someone who never experienced attention or validation as a child except when they were being sexually abused, would then learn to associate and equate love with sex or with a form of sexual abuse. Another example, someone with a controlling parent who received approval and validation only when they were being told what to do would then take on an unconscious pattern of thinking or equating controlling behavior by another person as a form of love. These dysfunctional patterns of reinforcement become the only frame of reference the child has, and so as an adult we are magnetically drawn to that same, abusive, unconscious pattern in our intimate relationships. When we meet someone who is controlling, we immediately have some feeling of being in love with this person which comes from our unconscious dysfunctional pattern of what we experienced as love during our childhood. Another example, a person that was sexually abused as a child will unconsciously choose a partner who is sexually abusive in some way or who is sexually dysfunctional, and they will be very attracted to this person.

THE QUESTIONS WE NEED TO ASK OURSELVES IN ORDER TO BE ABLE TO SEE, HEAL AND TRANSMUTE ANY ABUSE:

1. What does love mean to you as an adult?
2. What are your patterns of association with love that you experienced as a child?
3. Are these two answers the same or are they very different?

If these two definitions of love are distinctly different from one another, then you will know that what you experienced as love during your childhood, is most probably a reinforced dysfunctional pattern of abuse.

## HOW TO HEAL AND RELEASE
## YOUR PATTERNS OF ABUSE

1. Create a new personal definition of love based on the things you've learned, read, or experienced with healthy people, i.e. friends, teachers, therapists, business associates, etc.
2. Then compare what you knew or experienced as love during your childhood to your present, personal definition of love as an adult. If you meet someone with whom you are interested in having an intimate relationship, DO A REALITY CHECK of this potential relationship by doing the following:
   a. Consult with a therapist, counselor, or a neutral person who is not emotionally involved with you.
   b. Give clear, specific examples of interactions with this person in whom you are interested, and then ask the counselor or friend to compare these to the definition or information you have of either healthy, nurturing love, or the illusory love you experienced through dysfunctional patterns in your childhood.

Appyling this process will help you to get a clearer and more objective picture as to whether you are breaking the old dysfunctional pattern and attracting healthy, supportive, nurturing love into your life.

### INTERACTING IN AN INTIMATE RELATIONSHIP

There are times when we feel powerless and feel like we have no choice as we interact in some of these relationships. Many times we contract, and pull back, without really communicating our true feelings. The first step is to acknowledge to yourself that there is a challenge or conflict in your interaction with this person. Get in touch with what feelings are coming to the surface, and take a closer look at how these feelings are affecting you.

It may not be appropriate for you to open up a more intimate part of yourself until you are clear that the person with whom you are interacting is ready, open, willing, and capable of connecting with you on the same level of integrity, clarity and openness as yourself. Using your discernment, ask yourself if this relationship has a true and lasting potential for a healthy, balanced, and trusting interaction that is loving and supportive. The reverse can also be true. Do you trust yourself enough to be open with someone who may not have the same boundaries as you? Are you able to match or aspire to the same level of honesty, clarity, and integrity as your partner? Do you feel good and secure about yourself in relation to your partner, without putting them up on a pedestal?

Those of us who deal with major issues of setting up limits and boundaries in our close relationships, and always have to consider how much to allow someone into our personal space, are the people who have suffered and experienced some form of abuse in childhood and/or in an intimate relationship. Maybe there was a time, when we felt really vulnerable and needy and just couldn't say "NO", and so we compromised our integrity and self-worth by surrendering to a situation that we later regretted. There are times when we feel such a strong human longing for love and acceptance, that at times we lose our perspective and personal values, as we act more out of need rather than love. This is also an unconscious form of self-abuse. When we deny a certain feeling we are afraid to show or express, and judge it as bad, low, ugly, or shameful, we invite shame, criticism and repeated abuse into our lives. This form of denial and suppression creates even a greater split and polarization within our subconscious mind as our self-judgment is acted out, mirrored and amplified through our intimate relationships.

Being honest and real with your pain by facing and accepting it fully, and being able to show and express this pain with a close friend or partner by saying, "This is where I hurt" is perhaps the first step to creating an honest and healthy relationship. By not qualifying or judging your pain as either good or bad, you neutralize and dissolve the old subconscious emotional-identification patterns, and a new space is created for your your own loving self-acceptance and healing. REMEMBER: When feeling or experiencing emotional pain, BE FULLY PRESENT WITH YOURSELF. Be completely honest about how you really feel, without judging or putting yourself down. Develop greater trust and compassion for yourself, by following the seven step program for healing emotional abuse. (See page 50-56) **When someone else is opening up to you and sharing their most vulnerable feelings and personal experiences with you, even though it may not be in harmony with your standards of perfection or beliefs, are you still able to love them unconditionally in a nurturing gentleness without judging them or 'putting them down' in some subtle way?** This is probably the greatest challenge that we as human beings face in all our interactions and relationships. This is one of the most important lessons that the earth plane has to offer. How you care for your own level of self-worth and integrity, loving yourself for who you are and being loving and kind toward others, regardless of their personal beliefs or lifestyle, is an extension of your own level of self-acceptance and self-mastery. What makes this earth so unique is that it has such a variety and diversity of beings whose soul evolutions have such varying degrees of personal and spiritual development. Learning how to get along with one another, honoring another being's personal reality in a 'smorgasbord' of languages, beliefs, religious boundaries, tastes, habits, and addictions that differ from one another like night and day is the training ground for the development and evolution of the human soul. It is the training ground for realizing universal love.

**These human challenges provide us with tremendous opportunity for personal growth as we strive to evolve from the cocoon of a 'separate individual identity' to a 'collective, transpersonal' consciousness, of ONE GOD SELF, as ONE GLOBAL FAMILY united in Love.** Learning to adjust and relate to the mutable nature of human development, is to learn flexibility and the art of personal detachment. We let go of old beliefs and concepts in order to create a new, more loving space that enables our wholistic integration within the entire world as we lovingly interact with all the myriad forms of human relationships of which we are a part.

# 16

# THE PERSONAL SELF, THE TRANSPERSONAL SELF, AND THE UNIVERSAL SELF

In studying human relationships, I have become aware of three distinct patterns of identity that interweave with one another through our various interactions and communication with others. The personal self is the first and primary stage of our human development. It is concerned with our basic needs for survival, how we relate emotionally, mentally, sexually, and how we express ourselves in the physical world. The personal self is a direct extension of the development of the human ego. Its limitations and boundaries are defined in direct proportion to its perceptions and interactions with the external world. What creates our own personal identity, or our personal self are the influences of people around us. It starts at the moment of conception. During the time the fetus is in the mother's womb, it absorbs a lot of emotional patterns of the mother. As the child develops, parental influences, social environment and the culture in which the child is raised, all contribute to the development of the child's personal identity. A personal identity is formed by how the child is able to relate to its home environment as well as external stimuli. To include even deeper levels of soul memory, there are multiple sub-personalities from other lifetimes that interface with the soul's present personal experiences and development. How you interface with other people emotionally and personally is influenced by your belief systems and your personal perception of reality. This includes your habits, addictions, fears, traumas, pain, as well as positive reinforced experiences, how you see and feel about yourself, and the quality of validation you received from parents and peers during your childhood years. Another important aspect that contributes to the development of your personal identity is how you respond to your own self-imposed limitations, whether these are conscious or unconsciously created. How you personally handle life's many challenges also determines the strength of your personal choices which in turn help develop your identity.

## THE TRANSPERSONAL SELF

During the process of our personal transformation or healing, we learn to take a step back and become the witness and observer of our emotional interaction with ourselves and others. To facilitate our transformation and healing, we learn to detach ourselves from our reactive mind by not identifying with, or 'personalizing' our mental and emotional experiences as the only reality that is available to us. This accelerates our personal growth and allows us to process through challenging situations more quickly and more effectively. As we start to realize and become aware that there are other human beings that are also experiencing very similar challenges and lessons in life, we begin to learn compassion through developing a quality of love and detachment toward our own limited experience of 'me, mine, myself, and my own problems'. We begin to shift to 'ours', as we transform our own limited awareness of ourself into a more comprehensive, and inclusive relationship to the rest of life, humanity, and the cosmos. This level of awareness is known as the development of our transpersonal self. Being more open and receptive to other people's personal growth process, and becoming a loving, compassionate observer who is fully present and supportive, opens the door to your very own inner healing and the development of your transpersonal self.

YOUR TRANSPERSONAL SELF IS THE INTEGRATED ASPECT OF YOUR INDIVIDUAL SELF IN RELATIONSHIP TO THE WHOLE. **This process becomes part of your conscious, growing awareness, as your sense of Self and Identity evolves into a more expanded, collective, inclusive, all-embracing interaction with humanity and the life around you.** When you recognize and perceive that the person sitting next to you, IS a part of your greater SELF, and that everything that you perceive and experience around you is an extension of your Self, you are then relating on a more transpersonal level of awareness. This transpersonal aspect of your identity is always readjusting and redefining your relationship to the whole, as your awareness becomes more flexible and mutable to flow with the changing tides. When you become more conscious of how your thoughts, feelings, and actions are affecting the whole, your awareness expands to embrace the One Transpersonal Self of All Humanity. Reaching out to touch this part of yourself and humanity develops a higher quality of life on our planet, as our human potential expands to enfold the universal essence of all creation.

During deep inner states of meditation, the limited sense of my personal self dissolves, and I begin to experience a merging with various highly evolved beings of light and ascended masters on the inner planes. After practicing meditation for over twenty-two years, this has become an effortless reality and has truly expanded my limited human awareness of Self. These light beings can be your personal celestial guides, guardian angels, ascended masters,  or your Essence-Twin (Twin Flame). These beings are part of your soul evolution and are here to assist you in your spiritual development. As you begin to merge with these guardians and celestial guides, your own personal identity will start to shift and expand as you start to accept these beings as part of your evolving Self. This facilitates transpersonal communication between you and these beings of higher intelligence. This level of communication will serve to expand the quality of all your relationships. There may be people or friends who may no longer be appropriate and able to share and communicate on this level. When you begin to relate more on a transpersonal level with yourself and others, you will probably attract new friends and associates into your life who will share the same reality.  This becomes a truly uplifting and supportive communications network, as greater healing light flows into your reality and enlightened information is transmitted and mutually shared. This profoundly changes how you communicate and relate to the rest of the world. It also raises your own vibratory level of love and communication as all your relationships evolve into a deeper, more meaningful, and illumined reality.  This also enhances your self-worth, as the quality and integrity of your personal life is raised to a more enlightened state of Being.

## A SHARED MEDITATION TO EXPAND
## TRANSPERSONAL COMMUNICATION
Have you ever looked at someone up close and stared

into their eyes for awhile without taking away your gaze? After a while, you begin to see multiple personalities or different faces emerging as you focus on each other's eyes. This is a great exercise in developing transpersonal communication. Together with a partner, get in a comfortable seating position facing one another. Close your eyes. Take a few slow, deep breaths and contact your inner self. Give yourself permission to share your innermost self with the person in front of you. As you in-breathe, visualize white light filling your whole being. When both of you feel relaxed and ready, open your eyes and keep your gaze focused on the middle point above your partner's eyebrows (third eye). You are creating a powerful focus in the form of a pyramid with both of your eyes as the base of the pyramid, and your third eye as the apex. If you keep your gaze and attention focused on your partner's third eye, you will start to experience interdimensional communication that will unfold the multi-faceted aspects of you and your partner's transpersonal Self. You might see all kinds of different faces, perhaps some of them from other lifetimes, you may see lights, or a shadow-self surface in front of you. Whatever you see, just keep your heart open and go with the flow. Begin recognizing this person and everything you are perceiving through them as a part of yourself. This will transform your perceptions and experiences profoundly and you will notice a major shift of energy in your own awareness of yourself in relation to your partner.

The key word is to ALLOW YOURSELF TO EXPERIENCE AND WITNESS WITHOUT JUDGING WHAT YOU ARE SEEING. By embracing everything that you are perceiving in unconditional love, you will notice a major transformation and shift of all your judgments and fears as they dissolve and are replaced with loving acceptance of yourself. If the energy gets too intense, you may wish to close your eyes and retreat back into your own inner space until you feel rebalanced. Do this eye-gazing meditation only as long as it is comfortable for both of you. By allowing your partner to express their intimate self to you, a space of safety and acceptance is facilitated that will assist both of you to express yourselves more freely, without holding anything back. This will also help heal a mutual fear of rejection. Being able to express all aspects of yourself freely is very important in creating and maintaining a healthy loving relationship. If the person you are in a relationship with, has difficulty accepting these parts of yourself, then you are probably not with the right person. Don't hold back the depth and intensity of your feelings. The more open and free you are in expressing what's inside of you, the more you will expand the creative life essence of the universe.

### THE ART OF CREATIVE INTROSPECTION: EXPANDING YOUR TRANSPERSONAL SELF

As you learn to go more within, and tune into your inner self, you will come to a point of peace and stillness. This is a place where the mind begins to unwind, **and in deeper states of meditation, the mind becomes even more still to the point where you begin to release and let go of all your perceptions.** This is a form of re-training an overactive mind to retreat, and allow a deeper state of light and awareness to manifest. The deeper you go within and the more stillness you can absorb by letting go of the mind, the more clarity, illumination, and peace you will manifest. You may experience many thoughts speed by; just watch them, let them go, and don't try to control them by resisting them. Simply be aware of their presence, and stay focused on the light within. When your thoughts begin to dissolve, you will experience a new level of surrender and tranquility that will empower your whole being with greater light and awareness. Let all your thoughts and perceptions dissolve into the Light. Stay focused on the light within.

As you go even deeper, you may start to experience a profound and intimate communion with interdimensional beings of light such as your personal guides or celestial guardians. Allow yourself to receive their love and light as you expand your receptive capacity. During this process, you may experience the dissolving of your own personal identity and ego as you start to merge into even greater Light. This is a wonderful sign! What is really happening is an INTERFACING of energies between your human personality and your expanded I AM GOD PRESENCE. Go with the flow. Continue to open up more by surrendering your ego and merging deeper and deeper as you allow yourself to experience whatever level or degree of expansion you are capable of embracing at that moment. You will no doubt experience great joy and upliftment as you begin to experience the expansion and integration of your I AM Presence. You will feel less limited and trapped by your personal human ego-self, as the merging and interfacing continue to develop and evolve. Let your heart travel on wings of light into ever-expanding dimensions of love and infinity. You may meet a few other souls along your path that may assist you in the awakening, integration and reclaiming of your True Identity. These may be physically incarnate beings or celestial light beings that vibrate to a similar soul frequency as yourself. **As we reclaim our 'True Identity', learning to integrate this inner communion and bring it into physical expression on earth is what true mastery is all about.** THIS IS ALSO KNOWN AS SOUL EVOLUTION.

The great Tao flows everywhere,
both to the left and to the right.

The ten thousand things depend upon it;
it holds nothing back.

It fulfills its purpose silently
and makes no claim.

It nourishes the ten thousand things,
and yet is not their Lord.

It has no aim; it is very small.

The ten thousand things return to it,
yet it is not their Lord.

It is very Great. It does not show Greatness,
And therefore is truly GREAT.

. . . from a poem by
Lao Tsu

## THE UNIVERSAL SELF

As you become more proficient in anchoring your I AM Presence into physical reality, you will naturally tap into a more unlimited and universal aspect of your True Identity. The I AM Presence within you is an aspect of yourself that is connected to all of creation, to all of life, and to everything that exists in the universe. Your I AM Presence is never separate from your true and real Self. This light, this power, this Presence, awareness, intelligence, consciousness, call it what you will, is in every living creature, and is the only reality that remains constant. It is the very nature and essence of all existence and Life itself. This energy can neither be created nor destroyed as the brilliant physicist Albert Einstein exemplified through the equation $(E=mc^2)$.

**Universal energy is a vibration of consciousness that pervades and sustains all existence.** It is this spark of light within our soul that gives us life, and this same spark that ignites the fire of our soul journey into higher dimensions of light after the 'death' of the physical body. You cannot measure this spark by its size or appearance. It transcends time and space and yet it sustains the illusion of time and space. It also has the power and capacity to expand itself into whatever dimension it chooses. It is man's eternal quest to seek ways of becoming ONE with this spark, to understand its power and will, its intelligence and relationship to himself. Enlightenment dawns when man realizes that he is already ONE with this Essence, was, and always WILL BE. **The only difference between this supreme Power-Intelligence and Man is the separation within the mind of Man out of which the illusion of duality was born.** This was the symbolic and original 'temptation' of Adam and Eve as they ate of the tree of 'knowledge'. (i.e. the birth of duality–good and evil.) What remains to be healed and transformed are the veils of self-imposed denial and sub-concious oppression that obstruct the clear Vision and understanding of this universal life essence. By ac-knowledging your I AM Presence as a vital aspect of your self and working in harmony with this universal intelli-gence, your I AM Presence will allow you to access more clarity, healing, empowerment and self-realization. By making this focus a priority in your daily life, you will learn how to integrate this reality into all your interac-tions, whether they are personal, business-related, or spiritual. Even taking ten or fifteen minutes a day to sit and tune into this universal life essence within you, allows it to expand through you as it helps you to readjust any energy that is out of balance. One effective way to do this is to sit in meditation and become conscious of your breathing. Breathe in and out slowly, and just **allow** yourself to feel the life and light within you. Give yourself permission to explore a new part of yourself by staying open to new possibilities of awareness, as you let go of your concepts and expectations. When you start to commune regularly with this universal essence, you will expand the creative powers of your perceptions and visualizations to a whole new level of awareness. All ascended beings have evolved their human personality by first learning to freely express and integrate their transpersonal self into their physical and spiritual reality. This automatically raises the vibrational frequency of their mental, emotional, and physical body to a level of universal Being. Their true soul essence and purpose becomes fully activated and integrated into physical reality. At this level, their own personal identity is fully merged with the universal laws of creation. Their pro-jected intention, directed purpose and will is in total alignment and harmony with the power, will, creative expression and love of the highest intelligence in the universe. At this universal level, there is no more self-abuse or self-denial. There is a total and complete acknowledgment, surrender and merging with the essence of all BEING. The love nature (Pink Ray), intelligence (Golden Ray), and will-power (Blue Ray) are equally integrated and directed toward serving the light. The personal ego is surrendered to a greater Will  as the transpersonal self is firmly anchored in all  activities of daily life. This can be in the form of assisting others in their healing, enlightenment, developing more loving relationships, assisting artists and musicians to create great works of art and music, and many other constructive forms of communication and service to humanity. Any activity that assists humanity to evolve into a more whole, harmonious, loving, and illuminated Consciousness, becomes the focus of these great universal beings of Light.  Many of these beings also serve life on other planetary dimensions besides earth, as they assist the acceleration of love, light, and universal intelligence of other life forms.  When an individual realizes his or her soul purpose, the light energy within that soul will manifest in the consciousness and mind of that individual as an intelligent  Living I AM Presence. As the individual (personal self) soul merges and interfaces with this universal intelligence (I AM Presence), the integration that takes place gives birth to a whole new level of being that is known as the UNIVERSAL SELF. At this level of consciousness, you are ONE with all Beings, with all Life, with God.  This consciousness transcends the illusions of time/space and all duality and conflict of the personal, human self. At this point all your energy and light is directed toward raising the quality and vibration of all life (including your own) for the healing, enlightenment and liberation of humanity.

# 17

# THE INTEGRATION OF
# THE PERSONAL, TRANSPERSONAL
# AND UNIVERSAL SELF

The purpose of all relationships is to help us grow and evolve. **The challenges that are presented to us through relationships are there so that we may take another step toward expanding the love nature within our hearts through compassion and forgiveness as we heal all forms of abuse.** Relationships teach us how to share, how to give, how to receive love. They teach us how to be more trusting and open with ourselves and others. Relationships also make us aware of our limiting belief patterns and perceptions as we are challenged to see another point of view, or to see ourselves as others see us. All these challenges stretch our human potential for growth and mastery.

**If two souls vibrate to a similar frequency and purity of love, the potential personal challenges that surface at times appearing to threaten the ego, can be creatively utilized to accelerate our process of self-transformation and healing.** This can greatly enhance the quality of love, communication, intimacy, and integrity between any two people. As the purpose and goals of two souls are in alignment, the power, light and love that is generated through the mutual resonance of their harmonious interaction, can transform and heal any form of abuse that may come up. As transpersonal communication develops and becomes anchored and integrated within their relationship, the growth and awareness of both beings expands and awakens to embrace the universal essence of all creation. As both beings are fully aligned with the ONE, their combined energies have even greater power for healing and transforming not only their personal lives but the life around them as well. For a truly fulfilling and liberating human relationship on earth, **all three aspects of our identity** must be in harmony with one another, as we learn to communicate and relate on a more healthy, fulfilling, and wholistic level, integrating the various levels and aspects of our True Identity.

You can have fun with your personal self if you don't take it too seriously. Be playful with your inner child and enjoy your own unique personal essence and flavor, as well as your partner's. **To maintain a truly balanced relationship on this physical plane, the inter-personal level of communication and expression must be fully present and integrated with the transpersonal self.** This means that you learn to honor the **person** that you are, and the **person** that you are interacting with in a relationship as a beautiful, unique expression of creation. You love them for who and what they are, with all their habits, judgments, fears, hopes, aspirations, etc. **You love the inner child of their person, and at the same time you love them beyond their perceptions, beyond their own awareness and identity of themselves. This is true unconditional love in action.** This opens the transpersonal window that allows unconditional love to grow and blossom in the relationship. When you can love each other beyond your limited perceptions of one another, this becomes a true love that allows greater trust and intimacy. You are then loving not only the essence of that Being, but you are Love itself.

Learning to respect each other's personal identity is a vital factor in sustaining a healthy relationship. As boundaries and personal limits are defined, communicated, and mutually respected, it allows more trust to stabilize the relationship. However, in order to grow and expand within a relationship, you need room to grow and expand your own inner awareness of yourself by also expressing your **transpersonal identity**. Always leave room for each other to grow and evolve. **It is very helpful not to 'crystallize' another person by locking them into a fixed personality pattern. That kind of projection subtly impairs their growth.** Learn to distance yourself from your own personal perceptions and projections by focusing more on your own potential to expand the love essence within you. This will accelerate not only your own personal growth but will also assist all the people that you are interacting with.

Communication is the key to a healthy, loving relationship. Being real with your feelings without projecting or blaming another, is a vital factor in maintaining harmony and love in a relationship. If there is something that bothers you in your interaction with another person, or a feeling or emotion that needs to be expressed, instead of saying, "You're doing this to me! You're making me do so and so, ...it's all your fault!" Take another healthier approach by seeing your personal challenge as an opportunity for you to take full responsibility for keeping your personal space clear without projecting or blaming the other person for how you feel. A healthier, more functional approach would be to say, "This is my personal experience, this is how I feel and this is what is going on inside of me. Could you please help me to clear this energy ?" or, "How can we both help one another to clear this, by being more loving, kind, compassionate and understanding, by acknowledging and validating our own and each other's feelings, so we can heal the cause of this misunderstanding or abuse?" **There is great power in our verbal expression and how we communicate to one another.** We can accomplish this in a more positive way by first validating, acknowledging, and accepting our partner's feelings as well as our own. This creates a space for safety, self-acceptance, and healing of our inner child, as the cause and effect of any emotional, mental, sexual or physical abuse that created a particular pattern of dysfunction is gradually dissolved, healed, and released. Learning more compassion and love for one's own unhealed inner child, as well as for the unhealed inner child of others, opens new doors to heal those tender, delicate, vulnerable areas.

**One cannot move into a transpersonal level of communication with another, until all of these personal issues are dealt with openly, honestly and lovingly.** This is the point where most relationships fall apart. When the personal challenges of the human ego point to so much unhealed pain and wounds within the inner self, and this personal pain and anger gets projected on the other person, one cannot truly advance to the transpersonal level of relationship. **Some beings avoid their personal problems by trying to relate on a more transpersonal level with others as an escape from dealing with their**

**personal human issues**. However instead, they create even greater self-sabotage and self-denial by not facing their own personal, human issues.

Once you and your partner accept and realize that these personal challenges surface for your mutual growth and evolution, you will both be able to transform and heal any projections or expressions of abuse that manifest in your relationship. By taking a realistic approach of your evolving personal identities and making the commitment to really be open and honest with your human emotions and feelings, you will have opened a liberating door to your personal, as well as your transpersonal growth. Learning how to let another being into your intimate personal life and space, is the first step to start activating a transpersonal level of relationship. Instead of escaping from the problems and challenges of the personal self, you make room for an expanded version of your greater Self, as you open your heart to birthe, receive, embrace, love, and nurture this part of yourself reflected in your partner.

YOU THEN BECOME THE LOVE
THAT YOU SO MUCH DESIRE.

# PART IV

# THE
# SELF–HELP
# MANUAL

WITHIN YOU LIES THE SEED OF ALL CREATION.

ALL THE LOVE IS THERE.

ALL THE LIGHT IS THERE.

ALL YOU EVER WANT AND NEED

IS WITHIN THAT SEED OF LIFE.

THE KEY BEYOND BIRTH AND DEATH IS THERE.

THE DOOR IS READY TO BE OPENED.

**YOU ARE THAT DOOR.**

# INTRODUCTION
# TO
# SELF – HELP MANUAL

This self-help manual is designed as a convenient reference guide for you to access practical information for your self-healing and empowerment. Use it freely anytime you want to access more information on the following tools for your transformation, healing and spiritual expansion:

• THE FOUR BODIES OF HUMAN ENERGY
  (See Introductory Chapter, page 1)

• GUIDED MEDITATION TO ENHANCE YOUR SEXUAL
  EXPRESSION  (See Chapter 4, page 22)

• THE SEVEN STEP RECOVERY PROGRAM FOR EMOTIONAL
  ABUSE  (See Chapter 10, page 50)

• INVOKING YOUR "I AM" PRESENCE
  See Chapter 21, page 118)

• AFFIRMATIONS FOR SELF-EMPOWERMENT
  (See Chapter 22, page 124)

- A COMPREHENSIVE GUIDE TO ACTIVATING AND BALANCING THE EIGHT ENERGY CENTERS (CHAKRAS) IN OUR BODY  (See Chapter 23, page 129)

- ANCHORING YOUR LIGHT BODY THROUGH THE EIGHT UNIVERSAL LIGHT RAYS: Guided Meditations, Visualizations and Affirmations
  (See Chapter 24, page 137)

- THE NEW HEALING COLORS:  THE THERAPEUTIC APPLICATIONS OF COLOR, LIGHT AND GEMSTONES
  (See Chapter 25, page 183)

- INTRODUCTION TO COLOR THERAPY: DISPELLING THE ILLUSION OF GENDER IN COLOR THERAPY
  (See Chapter 26, page 194)

- TWENTY-SIX STEPS TO IMPROVE GLOBAL AWARENESS
  (See Chapter 31, page 204)

# 18

# THE FOUR BODIES OF ENERGY

(See Introductory Chapter, page 1)

# 19

## GUIDED MEDITATION
## TO ENHANCE
## YOUR SEXUAL EXPRESSION

See Chapter 4, page 22

# 20

# THE SEVEN STEP
# RECOVERY PROGRAM
# FOR HEALING EMOTIONAL ABUSE

See Chapter 10, page 50

# 21

# INVOKING
# YOUR "I AM" PRESENCE

"OH, I MUST TELL YOU ABOUT A DOCTOR'S DISCOVERY. HE
X-RAYED THE HUMAN HEART AND FOUND A FLAME OF
LIGHT INSIDE THE FIFTH CHAMBER, IN AN AIR TIGHT CELL.
HE X-RAYED THE FLAME THREE THOUSAND TIMES AND IN
THE FLAME HE SAW A **PERFECTLY FORMED DIVINE BEING**,
WHICH HE CALLED **THE REAL YOU.**"

**Walter Winchell**, Post
Credit Broadcast,
Ontario,Canada
(On file in Oxford University, England)

Within each living being there is a spark of light that
originally created the life form of that being. Call it a soul,
a Higher Self, God, a Higher Intelligence, etc. It is not the
purpose of this book to prove or justify the Presence of
this Supreme Being or Intelligence. Since knowledge is
limited to the relative nature and perception of the mind,
we need to look deeper within our own consciousness to
find some of the answers to the mysteries of life. We
cannot always find the answers that we seek through the
rational, logical interpretation and limited perception of
the human mind. Therefore, the challenge that we as
human beings face is to learn to surrender our limited
concepts of the universe and creation by tapping into an

invisible Essence that permeates all creation. As we begin to tune into our own inner universe, we realize that this very same essence that created us has also created everything else. As our spiritual quest deepens, our respect for all life and creation begins to expand as we fine tune our own inner universe. When we learn to awaken and expand our inner light, our capacity for love and understanding increases and we find a new level of intelligent communication within ourselves and with the world around us. Being in touch with that spark of light that created us and learning how to live in harmony with that Presence is the manifestation of true mastery. When Moses stood by the burning bush and asked God what His name is, the reply was **"I AM"**. This one single affirmation is perhaps the answer of all Creation, of All That Is, was and will Be. Knowing that **"I AM"** is to know the secret of life and the universe. It is the key of existence that opens the doors to all dimensions.

Your I AM **God Presence** is a living, active electronic light substance that is all-knowing, all-intelligent, and all-loving. It knows you better than you know yourself. It is that part of you that is the eternal witness of all your life experiences. It automatically records every single experience, thought, and feeling that you have ever had. It does not judge, criticise, or condemn. Just before physical death, many people experience a rapid sequential cinematic survey of their whole life. Everything is sped up, as they witness the 'playback' of all their recorded life experiences. Your I AM Presence is also known as your True Self, or God-Self. When we heal the separation of duality in our thoughts, perceptions, beliefs and concepts, we begin to heal the illusion of separation between our human and God Self. This healing of separation is the journey of human evolution.

Your I AM Presence is completely free from any human projections or perceptions. It is a pure, neutral and unqualified, radiant energy, until you begin to consciously qualify your actions, thoughts, feelings and emotions with love, asking the Intelligence of your own I AM Presence to guide all your actions into a higher level of perfection and freedom. Your I AM Presence is an all-intelligent, universal, electronic substance of pure Cosmic Light Energy. Once it is invoked or called upon, it begins to activate great powers of assistance to help you manifest your true potential. Learn to communicate with this sacred part of yourself, and observe the new levels of love and awareness that you will experience. As you learn to love this part of yourself more and more, greater love, healing and abundance will flow and manifest in your life.

Visualize your I AM Presence within your Heart. It lives in a tiny flame of light in the fifth inner chamber of your Heart. There is also a cylindrical beam (tube) of light extending from that heart chamber through the top opening of your head and crown area that extends up and through the silver cord (anthakharana) above your crown. Many beings experience rising up through this silver chord as they consciously travel out of their bodies, or have 'out of the body' experiences. It is also the vehicle and channel of light through which they return to their physical bodies. The same is true when we sleep at night and experience different levels of soul travel. We leave our bodies and travel to various places or dimensions, and in the morning we return through the silver cord back into our physical body.

The auric emanation of your I AM Presence contains all the colors of the Eight Universal Light Rays (see page 137) as well as other colors that are not visible to our human spectrum. As you learn about these eight light rays, you will learn how to activate the intelligent substance of electronic light energy within each ray in relationship to the energy centers (chakras) of your body. This will assist you in anchoring your Electronic Light Body, - your I AM Presence, into physical reality. Before you invoke your I AM God Presence, it is very helpful to do the following visualization and meditation. This exercise will greatly assist you in your interaction with the outer world, as it will enfold you in an electronic beam of light or shield of protection wherever you are.

## "TUBE OF LIGHT"
### MEDITATION and VISUALIZATION

Visualize yourself standing with your arms at your sides and your palms open. Visualize an electronic spiral of Violet Light starting at the bottom of your feet and moving all the way up to your crown, then spiralling back down, then up, all around your body until you are completely enfolded in an intensely brilliant tube of violet light. When you have sufficiently anchored this violet tube of light around you, begin to visualize a brilliant white light surrounding the violet tube of light. The brilliant white light completely envelops and surrounds the tube of violet light in the same tubular shape as the violet light. Hold this focus of the white tube of light until your whole being is filled and surrounded by this beam of white light. Then begin to affirm:

**"Beloved Mighty I AM God Presence:** Seal your Tube of Light that I now invoke from the Ascended Masters' Flame, in, through, and around me. Let it keep my Being Free from all misqualified Human Creation and projection, past, present and future.  I **AM** calling forth the **Violet Transmuting Flame and Fire** to blaze and transmute all misqualified human creation  in Freedom's Name, for I AM ONE **with my own God Flame.**"

This affirmation and visualization will create an invincible shield of protection in, through, and around you, as well as seal your energy from any astral forces or negative human projections. Use it daily, at least two to three times, and you will notice an increase of light, balance  and protection in your life.  Once you stabilize your focus and attention on your true identity, Your I AM PRESENCE will assist you  as you  begin to realize that **"Yes, I AM that I AM."**  I AM the Light, and I AM the Love, and I AM the Power to overcome all obstacles in my life through the very power of all that I AM."

That part of your I AM that you are starting to acknowledge begins to take on a new meaning once you start to qualify it with positive, healing affirmations and visualizations.  When you realize that everything you have ever wanted to be, is already part of you and exists within your I AM Presence (True Self), you begin to affirm the true meaning of I AM. I AM is that part of you that is the all-knowing, all-seeing eye of God, the Master, the teacher, the illumined Self, the witness, the observer, protector, sustainer, the loving, caring BEING that you truly ARE.  Remember that this part of you is never in judgment or criticism, but is all-loving, all-accepting, and all-caring. Your I AM Presence is a Living BEING of Pure Unconditional Love. Be aware of the power of the spoken word. Choose your words carefully for they have an immediate impact on your feelings, body, and emotions. Be careful not say, "I AM tired, or I AM sick." Rather say

"My body is feeling tired or sick." Never qualify your I AM with a negative since this will set up an instant projection that will manifest in the physical. Watch and become aware of how you qualify your energy, for your I AM Presence is like a blank screen that feeds back to you exactly the level of quality of information or suggestion that you input. This is one of the laws of universal creation.

On page 124, you will find a list of powerful and effective healing affirmations to assist you in manifesting your highest creative potential. Consult these affirmations whenever you need to transform limiting thoughts and feelings, or whenever you feel your energy is blocked. These affirmations will assist you in re-balancing, revitalizing and re-integrating your mental, emotional, physical and etheric bodies.

# 22

# AFFIRMATIONS FOR
# SELF-EMPOWERMENT AND HEALING

The following affirmations are created for your personal empowerment so that you can manifest your highest creative potential. Be aware of your feelings and thoughts as you repeat these affirmations. Quite often, during some of these affirmations, you may hear your subconscious mind reacting in a negative way to a particular affirmation by telling you, "NO, I don't really deserve love and happiness, or NO, I am not worthy to receive love, or NO, I'll never have that kind of relationship." When those thoughts and feelings surface, do not resist them or push them away. Allow them to surface freely so that you will become aware which affirmations you need to focus on more. Repeat these until you feel a full and total acceptance of that affirmation in your emotional body and your subconscious mind. Use these affirmations more often than the others, until you no longer encounter any denial or resistance in your feelings and thoughts. This process involves dissolving old, limiting patterns of identification in our subconscious mind associated with abusive behavior. The following affirmations, when practiced regularly, help dissolve these dysfunctional patterns of self-abuse.

Continue to accept these positive, new 'seed' affirmations that you are lovingly planting into your subconscious mind, as you clear out the cobwebs of "Oh, I can't, I shouldn't, I'm not good enough, Oh, this will never happen." As you **replace** these old limiting programs with the new positive affirmations, your subconscious mind will automatically store and absorb the new positive information, and eventually your thoughts and behavior patterns will readjust and transform. This will harmonize your emotions, bring more fulfillment, health, joy, happiness and success into all areas of your life. When you begin each affirmation with "**I AM**", make sure you emphasize the "**I AM**" with conviction, feeling, love and self-acceptance.

1. **I AM** THE FULFILLMENT OF ALL THAT MY HEART DESIRES.
2. **I AM** HAPPY TO TAKE TIME OUT TO WORK ON MYSELF.
3. **I AM** ATTRACTING LOVE WHEREVER I AM.
4. **I AM** TOTALLY WORTHY OF RECEIVING THE LOVE I DESIRE.
5. **I AM** LOVED AND ACCEPTED BY EVERYONE.
6. **I AM** ALWAYS LOVED FOR WHO AND WHAT I AM.
7. **I AM** AT PEACE WITH MYSELF.
8. **I AM** AT PEACE WITH THE WORLD AROUND ME.
9. **I AM** AT PEACE WITH GOD.
10. **I AM** THE HARMONIZING PRESENCE OF LOVE THAT FULFILLS ALL MY NEEDS.
11. **I AM** THE MASTERY I AM SEEKING.
12. **I AM** THE JOY, SUCCESS AND FULFILLMENT OF ALL THAT I DESIRE IN LIFE.
13. **I AM** MY OWN BEST FRIEND.

14. **I AM** LOVING AND IN HARMONY WITH ALL PARTS OF MY BODY.
15. **I AM** A RADIANT BEING OF LOVE AND LIGHT.
16. **I AM** THE TOTAL FULFILLMENT OF LOVE.
17. **I AM** AT ONE BEING IN A FEMALE BODY.
18. **I AM** AT ONE BEING IN A MALE BODY.
19. **I AM** TOTALLY COMFORTABLE IN MY FEMALE BODY.
20. **I AM** TOTALLY COMFORTABLE IN MY MALE BODY.
21. **I AM** AT EASE WITH BOTH MY FEMININE AND MALE ASPECTS.
22. **I AM** AT EASE AND ACCEPT MY SOFT, RECEPTIVE, ALL-EMBRACING, OPEN FEMININE NATURE, AS WELL AS MY STRONG, ONE-POINTED, CREATIVE, EXPRESSIVE MASCULINE ASPECT.
23. **I AM** IN HARMONY WITH MY ANDROGENOUS ASPECT.
24. **I AM** COMFORTABLE AND ACCEPT ALL THE FEELINGS THAT I EXPERIENCE.
25. **I AM** COMFORTABLE EXPRESSING MY EMOTIONS.
26. **I AM** AT EASE WITH MY EMOTIONS.
27. **I AM** AT ONE WITH MY FEELING WORLD.
28. **I AM** THE FULL AND UNCONDITONAL ACCEPTANCE OF ALL MY FEELINGS.
29. **I AM** UNCONDITIONALLY LOVING ALL THAT I FEEL.
30. **I AM** AT EASE BEING CLOSE TO SOMEONE OF MY OWN SEX.
31. **I AM** COMFORTABLE EXPRESSING MY AFFECTION AND LOVE FREELY.
32. **I AM** AT PEACE WITH MY SEXUAL DESIRES.
33. **I AM** THE FULFILLMENT OF ALL MY SEXUAL DESIRES.
34. **I AM** AT ONE WITH MY SEXUALITY.
35. **I AM** LOVING MY SEXUALITY.
36. **I AM** UNCONDITIONALLY LOVING ALL PARTS OF MY SEXUALITY.

37. **I AM** AT EASE WITH MY SEXUALITY AND FEEL COMFORTABLE EXPRESSING IT.
38. **I AM** THE PRESENCE OF LOVE HEALING ALL PARTS OF MY BODY AND SEXUALITY.
39. **I AM** THE PRESENCE RECEIVING PURE, UNCONDITIONAL LOVE INTO ALL AREAS OF MY LIFE.
40. **I AM** THE PRESENCE AND GIVER OF UNCONDITIONAL LOVE.
41. **I AM** THE ACCEPTANCE AND RECEIVER OF UNCONDITIONAL LOVE.
42. **I AM** AT EASE AND LOVE TO EXPLORE INTIMACY.
43. **I AM** FREE WHEN I EXPLORE INTIMACY.
44. **I AM** THE TOTAL ACCEPTANCE AND EMBRACE ALL ASPECTS OF INTIMACY.
45. **I AM** AT ONE WITH THE INTIMACY I DESIRE.
46. **I AM** TOTALLY WORTHY OF LOVE AND INTIMACY.
47. **I AM** OPEN AND FEEL GOOD ABOUT SHARING MY LOVE AND LIFE WITH A LOVING PARTNER.
48. **I AM** ATTRACTING ONLY LOVING ENERGY AND LOVING PEOPLE INTO MY LIFE.
49. **I AM** ATTRACTING THE PERFECT INTIMATE PARTNER INTO MY LIFE.
50. **I AM** ATTRACTING A PARTNER INTO MY LIFE THAT LOVES AND RESPECTS ME FOR WHO I AM.
51. **I AM** ATTRACTING A PARTNER INTO MY LIFE THAT RESPECTS ALL ASPECTS OF MYSELF AND MY PERSONALITY.
52. **I AM** ATTRACTING MORE LOVE AND SUPPORT FROM EVERYONE IN THE WORLD.
53. **I AM** SUPPORTED, LOVED, AND NURTURED BY THE UNIVERSE.
54. **I AM** LOVED AND SUPPORTED BY THE EARTH.
55. **I AM** THE RADIANT HEALTH OF MY BODY MANIFEST IN EVERY CELL, ATOM AND ORGAN.

56. **I AM** THE HEALING PRESENCE AND POWER OF GOD'S INFINITE LOVE AND LIGHT.
57. **I AM** GOD'S LIVING LOVE.
58. **I AM** ALL THE ABUNDANCE AND PROSPERITY I NEED IN LIFE.
59. **I AM** THE RICHNESS OF GOD FLOWING THROUGH ME AND THE USE OF ALL THE THINGS I REQUIRE TO EXPRESS MYSELF IN LIFE.
60. **I AM** LOVED BY GOD.
61. **I AM** THE FULFILLMENT AND LOVE OF ALL RELATIONSHIPS.
62. **I AM** THE TOTAL FULFILLMENT OF LOVE.
63. **I AM** THE FULL MANIFESTATION OF LOVE.
64. **I AM** LOVE.
65. **I AM** THE FULL ACCEPTANCE AND MANIFESTATION OF ALL THE POWERS OF THE BEING THAT I AM.
66. **I AM** TOTALLY LOVED AND ACCEPTED BY GOD.
67. **I AM** THE HARMONIZING PRESENCE OF LOVE WHEREVER I GO.
68. **I AM** THE RESURRECTION AND THE LIFE, AND THE PERFECTION OF MY DIVINE PLAN FULLY AND PHYSICALLY MANIFEST HERE ON EARTH NOW.
69. **I AM** THE LIGHT OF GOD THAT NEVER FAILS.
70. **I AM** THE ASCENSION IN THE LIGHT.

# 23

# A COMPREHENSIVE GUIDE TO ACTIVATING AND BALANCING THE EIGHT ENERGY CENTERS (CHAKRAS)

**BASE OF THE SPINE CENTER**
(First Chakra)
**ENERGY CENTER LOCATION:** Base of the Spine
**CORRESPONDING LIGHT RAY:** Crystal White Ray
(See page 142)
**COLOR and ACTIVITY:** RED
Survival, Primal Fire and Life-force Essence. Pure Energy and Vitality
**HIGHER OCTAVE COLOR and ACTIVITY:** CRYSTAL WHITE Cosmic Purity and Ascension
**NEGATIVE POLARITY:** Unconsciousness, Fear of Survival, Being Ungrounded
**GLAND:** Adrenals
**ASSOCIATED MUSICAL INSTRUMENTS:** Deep, low drums, Bassoon, Primitive Drum rolls (Polynesian, African, Samoan, etc.)
**MUSICAL KEYNOTE:** C
**CORRESPONDING ELEMENTS:** Earth and Fire
**CORRESPONDING PLANET:** Earth, Mars

**HEALING GEM-CRYSTALS:** Obsidian, Black Tourmaline, Hematite, Bloodstone, Garnet, Smokey Quartz

**AFFIRMATION:** "I AM the Presence of Cosmic Christ Purity in all my thoughts, actions and feelings. I AM the Vital Energy of God flowing into every cell, atom, and organ of my body. I now affirm and claim my birthright to maintain a healthy, loving relationship with my physical body and the earth. Abundance and nurturing are expanding within me now to fulfill my every need, as I use my life force to benefit and serve the planet and all of life around me.

**I AM THE ASCENSION IN THE LIGHT.**"

## SACRUM CENTER
(Second Chakra)

**ENERGY CENTER LOCATION:** Sacrum Center (between the base of the spine and the lower abdomen.)

**CORRESPONDING LIGHT RAY:** Violet Transmuting Ray (See page 147)

**COLOR and ACTIVITY:** RED-ORANGE
Regulates sexual functions, and generative organs. Contains creative and pro-creative life force energy.

**HIGHER OCTAVE COLOR and ACTIVITY:** VIOLET. Transmutation, Acceleration, Invocation, Freedom, and all New Age Enterprises. The color of the next 2000 year earth cycle.

**NEGATIVE POLARITY:** Abuse of sexual energy, desire to destroy and control through sexual manipulation.

**GLAND:** Ovaries, prostate, testicles

**ASSOCIATED MUSICAL INSTRUMENTS:** Rhythm instruments, marimbas, saxophone, electric bass guitar

**MUSICAL KEYNOTE:** D

**CORRESPONDING ELEMENTS:** Fire and Air

**CORRESPONDING PLANET:** Mars

HEALING GEM-CRYSTALS: Carmelian, Amber, Garnet, Red Jasper, Bloodstone, Dark-green Tourmaline

AFFIRMATION: "I AM the harmonizing Creative Presence of God balancing and uniting both my male and female polarity into wholeness. The creative, projecting aspect of my masculine self is in perfect harmony and alignment with my open, receptive feminine self". "I AM THE UNCONDITIONAL LOVE AND SELF ACCEPTANCE OF MY SEXUALITY. I AM A BEING OF VIOLET FIRE TRANSMUTING INTO THE LIVING PRESENCE OF GOD'S ETERNAL LOVE AND LIGHT."


## SOLAR PLEXUS CENTER
### (Third Chakra)

ENERGY CENTER LOCATION: Abdomen area, solar plexus
CORRESPONDING LIGHT RAY: Ruby-Gold Ray
(See page 151)
COLOR and ACTIVITY: ORANGE-YELLOW
Seat of our Emotions, solar energy, warmth, radiance, balanced expression and use of personal power and emotions. Exuberance. Love of Nature and the elements.
HIGHER OCTAVE COLOR and ACTIVITY: RUBY-VIOLET and GOLD. Universal Peace, Brotherhood, Ministration and Service to Humanity
NEGATIVE POLARITY: Anger, Fear, Greed, Jealousy, Judgment, Criticism and Condemnation
GLAND: Spleen
ASSOCIATED MUSICAL INSTRUMENTS: Guitar, Oboe, Viola, Cello, Piano, Clarinet, Organ
MUSICAL KEYNOTE: E
CORRESPONDING ELEMENT: Water
CORRESPONDING PLANET: Moon

HEALING GEM-CRYSTALS: Citrine, Topaz, Calcite, Malachite, Amber, Rhodochrosite, Chrysocholla.

AFFIRMATION: "I AM inbreathing the peace of God into every cell, atom and organ of my body and being. I AM at peace with myself and the world around me. I **AM The Resurrection and the Life and the Perfection of my Divine Plan fully and physically manifest on earth now."**

## THE HEART CENTER
(Fourth Chakra)

ENERGY CENTER LOCATION: Upper Chest area in Center of Breastbone.

CORRESPONDING LIGHT RAY: Pink Ray (See page 155)

COLOR and ACTIVITY: GREEN
Qualifying our feelings, actions and thoughts with Love and Self-Acceptance.

HIGHER OCTAVE COLOR and ACTIVITY: PINK
All-embracing Love, Mercy, Compassion, Forgiveness, and Acceptance. Unconditional Love for all of life and creation.

NEGATIVE POLARITY: Attachment to personal self and Ego, Selfishness, Envy

GLAND: Thymus

ASSOCIATED MUSICAL INSTRUMENTS: Harp, Flute, Violin, Piano, Cello, Zither

KEYNOTE: F

CORRESPONDING ELEMENTS: Air and Fire

CORRESPONDING PLANET: Venus

HEALING GEM CRYSTALS: Rose Quartz, Kunzite, Pink Diamond, Aventurine, Pink and Green Tourmaline

AFFIRMATION: **"I AM the living Presence of God's Love in Action.** The Love that **I AM** expands within me as I allow myself to feel more and receive the love that is already flowing within me. As I share this love with others, it enhances the quality of my life and the well-being of the planet. I AM **the Acceptance and Living Presence of God's Unconditional Divine Love.**"

## THE THROAT CENTER
### (Fifth Chakra)
ENERGY CENTER LOCATION: Throat, slightly above the hollow of the throat.

CORRESPONDING LIGHT RAY: Cobalt Blue Ray
(See page 160)

COLOR and ACTIVITY: ROYAL BLUE
Projection of Power and Creative Energy, Communication

HIGHER OCTAVE COLOR and ACTIVITY: COBALT-BLUE Manifestation of Divine Will, Expression of creative energy into physical form. Protection, Faith, Leadership ability, and Communication.

NEGATIVE POLARITY: "Lording it over", abuse of personal power through manipulating others for selfish purposes.

GLAND: Thyroid, Parathyroids

ASSOCIATED MUSICAL INSTRUMENTS: The Human Voice, Flute, Woodwinds

KEYNOTE: G

CORRESPONDING ELEMENT: Air, Wind

CORRESPONDING PLANET: Mercury, Chiron

HEALING GEM-CRYSTALS: Tanzanite, Blue Diamond, Celestite, Amazonite, Blue Sapphire, Gem Silica, Turquoise, Aquamarine, Siberian Cobalt Quartz, Blue Quartz, Blue Tourmaline (Brazil)

AFFIRMATION: **"I AM the Presence and Power of God's Will manifest in all my thoughts, feelings, and actions.** I allow myself to be guided by God's will as

**I AM** filled and recharged with the power, strength, vitality and protection of my own mighty I AM God Presence. **I now claim my power and authority to express God's will and love wherever I AM.**"

## THE THIRD EYE CENTER
(Sixth Chakra)

**ENERGY CENTER LOCATION:** Middle of forehead, between the eyebrows

**CORRESPONDING LIGHT RAY:** Emerald/Indigo Ray (See page 165)

**COLOR and ACTIVITY:** INDIGO Intuition, Healing, focusing our energy.

**HIGHER OCTAVE COLOR and ACTIVITY:** EMERALD GREEN/INDIGO. Healing, consecration, precipitation, focusing through the power of creative visualization. Visionary powers of clairvoyance and clairaudience. Developing our power of one-pointedness through meditation and visualization.

**NEGATIVE POLARITY:** Misuse of psychic powers, misguided fantasy, inaccurate illusory projections.

**GLAND:** Pituitary

**ASSOCIATED MUSICAL INSTRUMENTS:** Electronic music instruments, synthesizers, chimes, Tibetan bells, crystal bowls

**MUSICAL KEYNOTE:** A

**CORRESPONDING ELEMENT:** Air and Ether

**CORRESPONDING PLANET:** Neptune, Uranus

**HEALING GEM-CRYSTALS:** Phenacite, Sugelite, Azurite, Flourite, Amethyst, Sodalite, Lapis Lazuli, Indicolite, Emerald, Diamond, Clear Quartz

**AFFIRMATION:** "I AM **The Presence** manifesting all that I need in my life. I AM God's abundance flowing through me and the use of all things I require for my service to life. **I AM the Healing Presence and Power of God's Infinite Love and Light. I AM the Acceleration of the Elohim Where I AM.** I AM THE SPIRIT OF CONSECRATION blessing everything that I wish to bring into manifestation with the Love and Light of God."

## CROWN CENTER
### (Seventh Chakra)

ENERGY CENTER LOCATION: Top of the Head, crown area.

CORRESPONDING LIGHT RAY: Golden Yellow Ray (See page 172)

COLOR and ACTIVITY: Electric ULTRA-VIOLET Wisdom and Intelligence.

HIGHER OCTAVE COLOR and ACTIVITY: GOLDEN YELLOW interchangeable with VIOLET. Divine Wisdom, Discernment, conscious understanding and awareness of the universal laws of creation. Illumination and Enlightenment. Also respect for all world religions and people's spiritual beliefs.

NEGATIVE POLARITY: None

GLAND: Pineal

ASSOCIATED MUSICAL INSTRUMENTS: Electronic Synthesizers, and electronic sounds that facilitate interdimensional communication with celestial light realms.

MUSICAL KEYNOTE: B

CORRESPONDING ELEMENT: Ether and Air

CORRESPONDING PLANET: Jupiter, Uranus

HEALING GEM-CRYSTALS: White Diamond, Selenite, Clear Quartz, Phenacite, Heliodore.

AFFIRMATION: **"I AM the Illumination and Enlightenment of God's Love and Light in Action.** I AM the **Light within the Heart of God."**

## ETHERIC LIGHT BODY CENTER
(Eighth Chakra)

**ENERGY CENTER LOCATION:** Above the crown, through the opening of the silver cord (anthakharana)

**CORRESPONDING LIGHT RAY:** IRRIDESCENT MOTHER-OF-PEARL (see page 177)

**COLOR and ACTIVITY:** Irridescent Mother of Pearl. Integration

**HIGHER OCTAVE COLOR and ACTIVITY:** IRRIDESCENT MOTHER OF PEARL RAINBOW LIGHT interlaced with WHITE AND GOLD LIGHT. Integration and utilization of all the seven light rays. Activation of the Universal Self and full awareness of the soul plane of consiousness.

**NEGATIVE POLARITY:** None

**GLAND:** None. However, this light ray extends from the soul plane into the form of the human aura (etheric body) which is anywhere from several inches to several feet from the physical body, depending on the soul evolution of the individual.

**ASSOCIATED MUSICAL INSTRUMENTS:** The Music of the Spheres

**CORRESPONDING KEYNOTE:** B flat

**CORRESPONDING ELEMENT:** Ether

**CORRESPONDING PLANET:** Uranus, Venus and planets in the fifth, sixth, and seventh dimensions

**HEALING GEM CRYSTALS:** Mother of Pearl, clearest Quartz Crystal with irridescent rainbow inclusions

**AFFIRMATION:** "I AM the full activation and memory of my soul purpose manifest on earth now. I AM THE FULL ACCEPTANCE AND FULL USE OF ALL THE POWERS OF THE BEING THAT I AM PHYSICALLY MANIFEST ON EARTH NOW. I AM the Light of God that never fails. I AM THE ASCENSION IN THE LIGHT. Beloved I AM (3x)."

**ANCHORING YOUR LIGHT BODY**
*through The Eight Rays*

(See Chapter 24)

COLOR PLATE 1

# THE HUMAN AURA

*The following photographs were taken in one day.*
*Each photo represent a different focus*
*that was held during that time.*

*Holding loving, spiritual, thoughts*

*Focusing on love, with a rose*

*Focusing on mental clarity*

*Holding a selenite wand*

It's amazing to see how different thoughts and feelings
produce completely different patterns of color and light
within the human aura.

COLOR PLATE 2

# THE NEW HEALING COLORS
### (See Chapter 25)

INDIGO          VIOLET         COBALT BLUE

TURQUOISE    EMERALD GREEN    GOLDEN YELLOW

PASTEL YELLOW    PASTEL PEACH    ROSE PINK

LAVENDER

COLOR PLATE 3

# THE THREE PRIMARY RAINBOW COLOR SPECTRUMS
*Highest Purity, Highest Light Essence, and Most Healing*
(See Chapter 26)

RAINBOW LIGHT THROUGH A CRYSTAL

ABALONE SHELL

MOTHER OF PEARL

COLOR PLATE 4

**CHAKRAS SPHERES**

COLOR PLATE 5

**CRYSTAL GODDESS**

COLOR PLATE 6

**MUSIC OF THE SPHERES**

Color Plate 7

# AEOLIAH VISIONARY ART
(See Appendix)

ANGEL OF HEALING

ANGEL OF ILLUMINATION

ANGEL OF THE PRESENCE

CRYSTAL GODDESS

COLOR PLATE 8

# 24

# ANCHORING YOUR LIGHT BODY THROUGH THE EIGHT UNIVERSAL LIGHT RAYS and THE CORRESPONDING CHAKRA SYSTEM with Guided Meditations

The following pages contain a comprehensive and informative description, together with practical guidelines and applications of how to work with the Eight Universal Light Rays for our self healing and spiritual expansion. The nature and essence of each light ray is described in full detail together with a guided meditation and visualization to help facilitate our healing and empowerment. Each ray has a specific function and focus which is also represented by a corresponding group of cosmic beings including an Ascended Master, an Archangel, and an Elohim. The purpose of these cosmic beings is to facilitate the accelerated transmission and activation of each specific ray as we learn to utilize these rays in our daily, practical reality.

An Ascended Master is a cosmic being who has mastered the cycles of birth and death (the recurring wheel of reincarnation, also known as *samsara*) and resides in a radiant light body in a higher dimension, such as the fifth, sixth, seventh and beyond. These beings have mastered all of the lessons and challenges of the earth plane. Some of these Ascended Masters have had recent physical incarnations on earth as late as the nineteenth century. There are documented letters of some of these trans-Himalayan Masters such as Master Kuthumi, Master El Morya, and St. Germain in the British Museum. All three masters lived during the 1800's.

These Ascended Masters have fully realized their Christ-Conscious Soul Essence and have moved beyond this physical time dimension into a more enlightened and expanded reality.   These beings have fully dedicated their lifestream in serving the Light by assisting humanity and other life forms to accelerate their evolutionary process. They are now channeling their accelerated light energy, love and intelligence through many souls on this planet, so that these light workers can assist humanity during this crucial time of planetary transition into the next millenium. As the old world is crumbling, the new foundation for a higher quality of life on this planet is being anchored.  This is happening through the dedication and service of these cosmic beings and through the millions of light workers who have incarnated to assist this planet in the next vital step of her evolution and transformation.

The atomic structure of these Masters has been transmuted from the physical-cellular level to the electronic light frequency of the ascended light body; they have also mastered the balance between the masculine and feminine polarity. They are androgenous beings who have raised their love and light vibration to a more evolved frequency of universal intelligence. They communicate through sound, light, feelings and thoughts that are electronically transmitted from and through their light body via their heart, third eye and crown centers. They communicate telepathically with other cosmic entities as well as with human beings. An Ascended Master is no longer limited to a 'human personality'; their personal ego has been totally transformed into serving the Universal Light and Cosmic Intelligence of God. Many of these beings are in a cosmic, transpersonal state of awareness as they are merged with many other evolved Masters such as Jesus, Buddha, Krishna, Confucius, Lord Maitreya, the Maha-Chohan, etc.

They are trans-personal beings who still retain an individualized 'I AM PRESENCE' developed and refined through many lifetimes. This makes them unique in their own particular soul expression and vibrational frequency of Light. The purpose and service of these Ascended Masters is to assist each human being in realizing individual Mastery and Ascension during this crucial time on planet Earth. They have fully mastered the specific qualities and essence of the particular ray, or rays that they serve on. Each has the authority and freedom to command the cosmic use of that particular light ray to whatever service is needed for the development and evolution of life. When we align ourselves with an Ascended Master, it accelerates the vibratory rate of our healing and transformation. This alignment allows us to manifest with greater ease and perfection whatever we wish to bring into physical form. This level of attunement also purifies and expands our personal intention and will, so our co-creation can benefit all of life. It also teaches us

how to relate on a more transpersonal level of communication as we learn to align our hearts, minds and wills
with these loving, evolved Beings of Light.

A corresponding Archangel and an Elohim also serves
on each of these Light Rays. These beings of light work
intimately with the particular Ascended Master of each
ray to assist in the anchoring and expansion of that ray.
An Elohim is a perfected cosmic being who literally
'transmits, channels, and directs' these mighty currents
of light energy into physical manifestation. The will,
authority and intention of the Ascended Master is immediately serviced by an **Archangel** who, in turn, **refines
and fine-tunes our emotional and feeling body** so we
can receive the transmission through the Elohim. The
purpose of the **Elohim** is to transmit the perfected vibrations of will, light, love and the directed intelligence of the
Ascended Master into **physical form.**

As you become familiar with the eight light rays, their
qualities and practical applications, you will naturally
feel more connected to some than others. You may feel
attraction to a particular ray in which you are deficient.
For example, if you have a highly developed intelligence
(Golden Ray) and a developed heart center (Pink Ray)
but are weak in expressing your will, and you feel taken
advantage of by others, then working with the Blue Ray
would be very helpful and therapeutic in anchoring your
power and learning how to direct your will in relation to
others.

There is a guided meditation and visualization that
follows the descriptive application of each light ray.
When you start to practice these meditations, I highly recommend working with the double cassette

entitled"*ANCHORING YOUR LIGHT BODY through the Eight Rays*". (See Appendix) This tape was specifically created for the activation and anchoring of these light rays into physical reality. This recording will allow you to relax, let go, and receive this transmission effortlessly, and without interruption. The music on this recording was also created and carefully chosen to help in the activation and in the anchoring process of the light rays in relationship to the eight energy energy centers (chakras) of the body. These vital energy centers control the function of our endocrine system which in turn regulates the process of metabolism, blood pressure, breathing, and the nervous system.

Before you begin your activation of these light rays, I recommend first familiarizing yourself with each ray. Study the page and information on each light ray until you become aware of the different qualities and applications of each ray. As you familiarize yourself more with the specific quality and light frequency of each ray, it will assist you in activating your process of creative visualization. Remember that each light ray is an electronic light frequency and is different from pigment. When you visualize a pure rainbow, you begin to see the actual **light frequency** that emits these color vibrations. This is also true of the light rays except that they are much more concentrated, brilliant and much more powerful than the rainbow light we see on earth. **As you become more aware of these cosmic light rays, start to visualize them as vibrant, electric, colored light of the most brilliant, rainbow spectrum. Be aware that these light rays carry electro-magnetic currents of specific, directed forms of universal intelligence that activate the transmission of interdimensional telecommunication between earth and the starry heavens.**

It is also helpful to consult the GUIDE TO ACTIVATING THE EIGHT ENERGY CENTERS (Chakras) (See page 129) This will also provide you with cross-reference information on the relationship between the Eight Cosmic Light Rays and the corresponding Chakras, as well as the affirmations, gemstone therapy, and polarity of each energy center. As you begin to activate each ray, it will automatically adjust the balance within the corresponding energy center (chakra) in your body associated with that particular light ray.

## THE EIGHT UNIVERSAL COSMIC LIGHT RAYS

### THE CRYSTAL WHITE RAY

CORRESPONDING ENERGY CENTER: BASE OF SPINE
    (See page 129)
PRESIDING MASTER: SERAPIS BEY
ARCHANGEL: GABRIEL
ELOHIM: ASTREA
QUALITIES and FOCUS OF RAY: Cosmic Christ Purity, Clarity, Self-discipline, and the Activation of the ASCENSION.
CORRESPONDING GEMSTONE: WHITE DIAMOND, QUARTZ CRYSTAL, SELENITE, WHITE SAPPHIRE, WHITE ZIRCON, ULEXITE, DANBURITE

Since white light contains all the colors of the rainbow spectrum, it is one of the most effective rays for clearing, purifying, and raising our energy level to a higher vibration of light and harmony. The base of the spine is the very foundation of our physical body. As we visualize filling and clearing our 'basement' with radiant white light, we then facilitate more pure and clearer energy flowing upward throughout our whole body without obstruction. As radiant health is a reflection of all energy centers integrated and in harmony with one another, it is vital to first clear the base of our spine center and fill our foundation with radiant white light so this center can transmit and channel this flow of white light energy throughout our entire body, nourishing our cells, organs, glands, tissues and nerves with its pure, life-sustaining energy. The purity of the Crystal White Ray will adjust any imbalances in the mental, emotional, and physical body. Your body will automatically absorb whatever colors from the white light spectrum that it needs most for its balancing and healing. This is another reason that white light is a universal focus in any spiritual healing or transformational process.

Another important quality of the Crystal White Ray is the activation of **ASCENSION**. Ascension is a sacred process of release and transformation that occurs when the human soul becomes liberated from the physical body and no longer chooses or needs to incarnate on the earth plane. These liberated souls choose to continue their spiritual evolution in higher dimensions of Light and Universal Love. Any being who has accomplished their Ascension truly becomes an Ascended Master. These Beings usually live in the fifth dimension and beyond. As their lives are dedicated to serving life on more expanded spirals of ecstacy, joy and Divine Love, they are able to manifest and co-create instantly whatever Vision they may have without any effort or obstacle. As their feeling world has become more perfected, their thoughts are able to instantly produce a desired manifestation. Their mind and heart have become so purified that only the most loving, clear intentions and will are projected into form as radiant light energy.

As we align ourselves with an Ascended Master, it speeds up our own vibratory rate so we can accomplish greater works of healing, service and illumination to assist humanity as well as ourselves. This process of co-creation allows us to manifest more quickly and effectively, with greater ease and perfection. It also purifies and expands our personal intention and will to a higher level of love and service.

## INVOKING and ACTIVATING
## the CRYSTAL WHITE RAY
GUIDED MEDITATION AND VISUALIZATION

The following Eight Ray Meditations and Visualizations with music can be found on a double cassette, entitled, *ANCHORING YOUR LIGHT BODY through the Eight Light Rays* (See Appendix). This double cassette is highly recommended for the following light ray meditations, as it will allow you to relax and just receive this interdimensional transmission of light and music without effort. Find a comfortable seating position, preferably in a half-lotus, or just sitting in a simple flat chair with spine erect.

Breathe in white light into your heart center. Then slowly exhale white light until it fills your whole aura. As you inbreathe the white light into your heart, sustain your breath and absorb this white light into your heart before you slowly exhale. Do this for about one to two minutes. When you feel enough white light surrounding your body, bring your attention to the base of your spine.

Visualize a circular beam (or tube) of brilliant white light descending from your heart center into the base of your spine. This beam of white light is filling the base of your spine with scintillating, sparkling, diamond-white light energy. Feel a tingling warmth activate your base center with radiant light energy. As you bring your attention down into the base of your spine, the sparkling, white light turns into a brilliant, sparkling, diamond-white, rainbow light. It begins to spiral upward through the beam of white light, spiralling around your sexual organs, then up into your abdomen, (solar plexus), then moves up to surround your heart center with sparkling, rainbow laser beams of white-diamond light, enfolding each chakra (energy center) with its brilliant light essence. As it spirals around your heart, it continues to spiral upward into your throat area encircling and spiralling within and around your whole neck area, filling your throat and neck with the brilliant white diamond light. As the spiralling light continues upward, it moves up into your third eye, opening and expanding your inner vision with the brilliant diamond essence. Your third eye is tingling with the brilliant white light, and sparks of rainbow, laser light beams emanate from your third eye as you witness this brilliant expansion of light.

The activation you are now experiencing in your third eye starts to move up even higher into your crown, surrounding your entire head and brain with the spiralling white-diamond light. It is moving faster and faster around your head, as the light frequency is accelerating, bringing greater illumination and joy into your crown center. As you feel your crown opening, that same spiral of light begins to spiral downward in an accelerated momentum, through the beam of white light, into your third eye, throat, heart, abdomen, genital area and back to the base of your spine. As soon as it reaches your base center, it starts to spiral back up through all your energy centers, up and down, in an accelerated momentum of spiralling light until the very center of your body becomes a vibrating beam of light with increasing spirals of white-diamond, rainbow light. Your whole body is fully illuminated from within as the radiant essence of pure white light is activated and anchored into your physical body. Feel the purification of all the energy centers in your body as they are cleared and cleansed by the rainbow laser beam of brilliant spiralling white-diamond light. Allow this light energy to flow to whatever part of your body needs it the most. Let your body absorb the light essence where it is needed.

As all the vital energy centers (chakras) along your spine are being cleared and purified, your whole body begins to take on a radiance all of its own. Bring your attention into the palms of your hands and feel radiant white light emanating from them. Slowly extend your arms outward with palms up in a receiving mode. You are now becoming the transmitter as well as the receiver of this radiant light energy. Place yourself in a large crystal pyramid of white light. This pyramid is stabilizing the electronic flow of white light energy and is helping you to absorb and contain it as well as to strengthen and amplify your aura so you can retain this transmission of light within your physical body. Feel how comforting it is to have this large, crystalline, white pyramid all around you, as you re-absorb the white light essence into your body and let it circulate wherever it is needed. Being inside this crystalline pyramid of Light is helping you to ground and stabilize the white light energy you have invoked. When you like, you can bring your arms and hands back into your lap with palms up and open.

AFFIRM: "I AM GOD'S PURITY MANIFEST IN MY BODY, MIND, FEELINGS, ACTIONS AND THOUGHTS. I AM THE ACTIVATION OF COSMIC CHRIST PURITY. This Presence of Light is now being permanently anchored within all the cells, atoms and organs of my body, sustaining and nurturing the life within them in perfect radiant health. I AM THE PERFECT RADIANT HEALTH OF MY BODY MANIFEST NOW. I AM THE ASCENSION IN THE LIGHT. BELOVED I AM."(3x)

As you accept these affirmations, a golden light appears around your crystalline, white pyramid. As you slowly return into physical consciousness, the crystalline pyramid of white light begins to dissolve as it merges into the golden light all around you. You are comforted and nurtured by this soft golden radiance that surrounds you. This Golden Radiance of Light is now being permanently anchored in all the cells and atoms of your body. As you begin practicing this and the following light ray meditations regularly, you will notice a major transformation in the quality and vibrational frequency of your energy. This will enable you to more effectively adjust any energies that are out of balance.

## THE VIOLET TRANSMUTING RAY
CORRESPONDING ENERGY CENTER: SPLEEN AREA
(Below the solar plexus- See page 130)
PRESIDING MASTER: ST. GERMAIN
ARCHANGEL: ZADKIEL
ELOHIM: ARCTURUS
QUALITIES and FOCUS OF RAY: TRANSMUTATION, ACCELERATION, FREEDOM, and all New Age Enterprises. It is the cosmic light ray for the next 2000

year cycle. Rhythmic invocation of the spoken word,
i.e. affirmations, etc.
CORRESPONDING GEMSTONE: AMETHYST, SUGILITE,
FLOURITE, VIOLET SAPPHIRE.

As violet is the fastest-vibrating light frequency in the
color spectrum, it has the greatest power and capacity to
clear, transmute and dissolve negative patterns from our
bodies and aura. The Violet Transmuting Ray is a most
effective tool in helping to clear old, karmic patterns from
the past. It acts as a powerful laser beam that dissolves
and cuts through the self-imposed obstacles of our human
creation and sets it free.

TRANSMUTATION is a process that dissolves crystallized, limiting, belief patterns and mental-emotional
blocks that have limited our full awareness and expression of our true Self (I AM Presence). As the process of
dissolving is initiated, an atomic re-structuring and re-
patterning of self-abusive thoughts and energies begins
which transforms our being into God's original blueprint
of perfection. An original state of Grace is re-established
during this transmutation process, much like the ancient
alchemists who were able to convert base metals into
gold by raising the atomic structure and frequency of the
denser metals into a more refined state. Calling on the
Ascended Master ST. GERMAIN to assist you in this transmuting process will greatly empower your ability to
anchor this light ray into your life wherever and whenever it is needed. Use it freely to clear your thoughts,
emotions, personal relationships, and to re-balance your
sexual energy. You may have noticed how popular this
violet color has become in the fashion industry the last
seven years or so. Wearing clothes of this color will also
help activate this light ray. Installing an ultra-violet light

bulb into your bathroom (in your shower) or bedroom, will also raise the energy and vibration of your environment.

The Violet Ray is also the ray of Freedom. All New-Age businesses and enterprises are overshadowed by this ray. The process of rhythmic invocation such as invoking your I AM Presence and repeating your affirmations in a rhythmic manner together with your breathing is another focus of the Violet Ray. This rhythm steps up the frequency of your affirmations and the process of acceleration is facilitated. Visualizing the Violet Flame spiralling in, through and around you is one of the easiest and quickest ways to clear your energy field and environment.

## INVOKING and ACTIVATING
## THE VIOLET TRANSMUTING RAY
### GUIDED MEDITATION AND VISUALIZATION

Center yourself for a minute and just get in touch with your I AM God Presence in your heart center. Invoke the Presence and assisance of Master St. Germain, Archangel Zadkiel and the Elohim Arcturus:

AFFIRM: "Beloved I AM God Presence, Beloved St. Germain, Archangel Zadkiel and Beloved Elohim Arcturus: BLAZE YOUR VIOLET TRANSMUTING FLAME AND FIRE IN, THROUGH AND AROUND MY ETHERIC, MENTAL, EMOTIONAL AND PHYSICAL BODY. Enfold them in spirals of ever-expanding and ever-increasing momentum of the Violet Flame until all my energy centers are cleared, cleansed and purified of all misqualified human creation."

Ask that any blocked energy within you, that you wish to have cleared and released, be completely transmuted and dissolved during the violet flame invocation and ceremony. Get in touch with what area in your life needs the most clearing, whether it is emotional, physical, mental, financial, or a personal relationship. Then visualize the violet ray and flame blaze into those areas dissolving and transmuting the blocked energy. We will now proceed by doing the 4-Step Breathing Exercise (See page 6) to clear and transmute our mental, emotional, etheric and physical bodies.

As you **inbreathe,** focus on the top of your head and aura (Etheric Body) and **AFFIRM: "I AM INBREATHING THE VIOLET TRANSMUTING FLAME INTO MY ETHERIC BODY".** Visualize the top of your head and your whole aura being permeated with this violet light.

As you **sustain (hold) your inbreath,** bring your attention to your head and crown (Mental Body) and **AFFIRM: " I AM ABSORBING THE VIOLET TRANSMUTING FLAME INTO MY MENTAL BODY."** Feel the violet light dissolve and clear your mind and brain of all blocks and obstructions.

As you **slowly exhale,** bring your attention to your solar plexus (abdomen–Emotional Body) and **AFFIRM: "I AM EXPANDING THE VIOLET TRANSMUTING FLAME INTO MY EMOTIONAL BODY."** Visualize the Violet Light moving down into your solar plexus area, clearing and dissolving imbalanced emotional patterns.

After exhaling, **hold your breath** and bring your attention to the base of your spine (Physical Body) and

AFFIRM: "I AM PROJECTING THE VIOLET TRANSMUTING FLAME INTO EVERY CELL, ATOM, AND ORGAN OF MY PHYSICAL BODY." Feel the life force of your physical body expand as you visualize this violet light entering your body, recharging all your cells and organs to a more balanced activity. Feel the momentum of the violet transmuting ray and flame send sparkles of violet light all through and around you. You are now bathing in the shimmering essence of the violet transmuting flame as it continues to spiral in, through and around you, lifting the accumulation of human creation from your whole being, raising its atomic structure to a more balanced and perfected state.

As this Violet Light pours through you, AFFIRM your unity with your I AM God Presence: "I AM THE LIGHT OF GOD THAT NEVER FAILS. I AM A BEING OF VIOLET FIRE, TRANSMUTING INTO THE LIVING PRESENCE OF GOD'S LOVE AND LIGHT."

## THE RUBY-GOLD RAY

CORRESPONDING ENERGY CENTER:   SOLAR PLEXUS
  (See page 131)
PRESIDING MASTER: CHRIST, LADY NADA
ARCHANGEL: URIEL
ELOHIM: PEACE and ALOHA
QUALITIES AND FOCUS OF RAY: UNIVERSAL PEACE,
  Service to Humanity in carrying out God's Divine
  Plan and the Reverence for all Life. Activation of the
  RESURRECTION RAY.
CORRESPONDING GEMSTONE: RUBY

True peace comes from within. The choices that we make always come from within our own will and desires. It is much like tuning into millions of radio wave frequencies. We can choose from trillions of different channels. Existing within these broadcast frequencies (light and sound as intelligence) is a tremendous range of vibration and information which can be either beneficial or detrimental to our physical, mental and emotional well-being.

Again the kind of energy or vibration you choose to accept into your being and aura determines your present state of consciousness. If you wish to experience and stabilize a deeper and more profound union and One-Ness with your Inner Self, it is wise to choose vibrations and people that will support your healing process and spiritual growth. **True Peace comes when we have healed the cause of all self-abuse, until we are no longer the victim of an unconscious, uncontrollable effect.**

When we nurture our body, mind, and emotions with thoughts that are loving and kind, we begin to heal the subconscious patterns of self-abuse. This nurturing process opens the door to our inner healing, allowing the space for a true inner peace to stabilize in our life. All forms of spiritual service to life and humanity through ministration and devotion to God by serving the light is the main focus of the Ruby-Gold Ray. This Ray also expresses a profound respect and reverence for all Life. It also represents the Activation of the RESURRECTION FLAME. The following guided meditation and visualization will assist you in stabilizing this inner peace through the Activation of the Resurrection Flame.

## INVOKING and ACTIVATING
## THE RUBY-GOLD RAY
GUIDED MEDITATION AND VISUALIZATION

As you inhale, breathe in the ruby-golden light and anchor it into your heart. Hold it there for a few seconds and as you release your breath, breathe out golden light and visualize it enfolding you in its radiant warm glow. (Do this for one to two minutes) All your cells are drinking in these warm healing rays of ruby-violet and gold. Your whole body feels warmer and more relaxed now as you surround yourself with these healing rays of peace and tranquility.

Place your hands palms down on your solar plexus (abdomen area). Let go of all effort and just allow yourself to feel the healing energy of your hands. Inbreathe the Ruby-Violet Light into your abdomen. Hold your breath for a few seconds as you fill that area with the ruby-golden ray. Exhale golden light. Feel your whole aura expand into the radiant essence of this inner peace. Empty all your thoughts and concerns into this gentle waterfall of peace, allowing it to enfold you in its soothing, tranquil energy. Bathe in its tranquil waters and refresh yourself in the calm and soothing balm.

**AFFIRM: "I AM AT PEACE WITH MYSELF AND THE WORLD AROUND ME.** I AM THE RADIANT PRESENCE OF GOD'S PEACE FLOWING IN, THROUGH, AND AROUND ME."
As you say this affirmation, all the cells, muscles, organs and nerves in your body respond as all tension and stress in those areas is completely dissolving. Place your hands back on your lap with palms up. Now do the 4-Step Breathing Exercise to stabilize Peace into your physical, mental, emotional and etheric bodies:

As you **inbreathe, AFFIRM: "I AM INBREATHING GOD'S PEACE INTO MY ETHERIC BODY."** Visualize the ruby golden ray of Peace enfolding the top of your head and your aura.

As you **hold your inbreath, AFFIRM: "I AM ABSORBING GOD'S PEACE INTO MY MENTAL BODY."** Visualize your entire head and brain fill with the light of the ruby golden peace."

As you **slowly begin to exhale, AFFIRM: "I AM EXPANDING GOD'S PEACE INTO MY EMOTIONAL BODY."** Visualize the golden-ruby light filling your whole solar plexus with its healing comfort and warmth.

As you **sustain (hold) your exhalation, AFFIRM: "I AM PROJECTING GOD'S PEACE INTO EVERY CELL, ATOM, TISSUE AND ORGAN OF MY PHYSICAL BODY."** Feel the ruby golden ray of Peace penetrate into all the cells and organs of your physical body.

**Repeat this 4-Step Breathing Exercise several times for approximately five to seven minutes.** You are now completely centered and your energy is balanced and whole. You rejoice in the gift that you are learning to give to your Self. You feel great reverence for the peace and life within you as well as for all life. Know that this great reverence for all life is your key to greater harmony and peace. **AFFIRM: "I AM THE RESURRECTION AND THE LIFE AND THE PERFECTION OF MY DIVINE PLAN PHYSICALLY MANIFEST HERE ON EARTH NOW."** Practice this particular affirmation often, as it will help you to anchor and stabilize your I AM PRESENCE into physical manifestation.

## THE PINK RAY

CORRESPONDING ENERGY CENTER: HEART
(See page 132)
PRESIDING MASTER: LADY ROWENA, PAUL THE VENETIAN, AEOLUS
ARCHANGEL: CHAMUEL
ELOHIM: ORION
QUALITIES and FOCUS OF RAY: All-embracing UNIVERSAL LOVE for all Life and Creation, Compassion, Mercy, and Forgiveness.
CORRESPONDING GEMSTONE: ROSE QUARTZ, KUNZITE, PINK DIAMOND, PINK OR WATERMELON TOURMALINE, MORGANITE, PINK SAPPHIRE, RHODOCROCITE, LAPIDOLITE, RHODONITE

Once you have a Vision or goal and you are clear in your intention-purpose, and have learned how to direct that goal with the clarity of wisdom, your third step is to qualify the desired manifestation with love. No manifestation can be of lasting value unless it is qualified with the FEELING OF LOVE. There is a certain quality and depth of **feeling** and **surrender** involved in channeling this love energy toward a directed purpose or goal. Love is the creative life force of the universe. The key to any form of mastery is to learn the balanced use of love (PINK RAY), together with directed will-power (BLUE RAY), balanced with wisdom and discernment (GOLDEN YELLOW RAY). To have a highly developed will-power and intelligence is not enough to sustain a manifestation that will be of lasting value to humanity. It is the love energy within any given purpose or goal that brings lasting value and benefit to all of life. In any artistic or creative expression, whether it be a ballet, a piece of music, poetry, drama, or healing, what really moves people deeply is the quality

and depth of love that they experience through the per-
former, artist, or healer. This quality of love becomes
infused into their creative artistic expression.

The act and capacity to unconditionally love, embrace,
and nurture all life and creation is the feminine aspect of
God's Love. **The ability to** FEEL and express through our
feeling world is another highly developed quality of the
Pink Ray. Allowing yourself to FEEL, to be open and
vulnerable, creates an opening in your heart for more
love to flow in. For true mastery in any dimension, both
the masculine principle of projected power-will and
wisdom must be in equal balance and harmony with the
feminine aspect of all-embracing love, mercy, compassion and forgiveness. Learning to be receptive and open
to receive Love is a very important aspect of the Pink Ray.
Learning to be more open, and creating the time and
space for inner nurturing, allows the universal love energy to flow more freely through you, making your life
more harmonious, more meaningful, and more fulfilling.
During the following meditation you will learn how to
expand the Pink Ray of Divine Love into your life.


**INVOKING and ACTIVATING
THE PINK RAY**

GUIDED MEDITATION AND VISUALIZATION
As you continue breathing in and out slowly, start breathing in a soft, pastel, pink light into your heart. As you
inbreathe this pink light into your heart, hold it there for
a few seconds and allow the pink light to spread throughout your entire chest area. As you exhale, exhale a soft
pink golden light that begins to fill your aura and the

space you are in. As you continue this breathing exercise, the environment around you is slowly being filled with the soft pink-golden radiance and a gentle space of comfort and safety is now enfolding you.

Invite your I AM God Presence into your heart. Allow this Presence into your whole body now. Visualize this presence as a tiny flame of golden-white in your heart as it expands and fills your whole body with its soft loving energy. Allow God in you to occupy the same physical space as yourself. Visualize the white-golden light of your God Presence merge with you and your body. As you let go of your mind and control, allow yourself to SURRENDER AND FEEL the Presence of God within you as your very own Being. The key word is to **ALLOW**, ALLOW, and ALLOW yourself to be enfolded by this loving Presence which is the REAL YOU.

As you continue inbreathing the pink light into your heart, hold your breath and hold that light for a few seconds and expand it now throughout your whole body. Continue exhaling the pink-golden light and inbreathing the pink light into your heart, and then expand it until it fills your entire body with pink light. Your whole body feels softer as the pink light gently moves from your heart up into your throat, your head, then back down into your heart, your chest, your arms, hands, your stomach, your solar plexus, genital area, your thighs, legs, and feet. Feel this pink light circulate throughout your whole body, filling it with the radiance of the Pink Love Ray. Slowly bring your attention back to your heart center and visualize a white-golden flame in its center with soft pink light glowing all around the flame. As you focus on this flame, the soft pink aura around the flame begins to glow a deeper pink, emitting laser rays of pink, rainbow light from your heart like a brilliant, pink diamond. Allow these laser rays of pink rainbow light to enfold your heart and body in a gentle caress, clearing away all resistance, tension and pain.

At this time, you may wish to call upon the Ascended Master **Lady Rowena** or **Beloved Aeolus, Archangel Chamuel** and the **Elohim Orion** to assist you in clearing any energies within your heart center that are not in alignment with universal love. This is a great opportunity to clear any hurt, pain, or old accumulation of blocked, 'stuck' energy in that area.

Begin by AFFIRMING: "I AM THE HEALING PRESENCE AND POWER OF GOD'S INFINITE LOVE AND LIGHT." Repeat this powerful affirmation as you breathe in and out, at your own speed. "I AM THE PRESENCE OF LOVE and FORGIVENESS, transmuting all doubt and fear into God's Living Light and Love. I AM THE HEALING PRESENCE AND POWER OF GOD'S INFINITE LOVE AND LIGHT. (3x) I AM THE FLAME OF LOVE AND FORGIVENESS RELEASING ALL that is not in alignment with Universal Love and Harmony from my body, aura and being. I AM THE PRESENCE OF LOVE filling these spaces with the radiant light of God's Love."

Continue visualizing the white-golden flame in your heart expand as the laser beams of pink-rainbow, diamond light sparkle from your heart center, filling your entire being with its shimmering radiance. As you focus on the white-golden flame in your heart you begin to notice that the flame is now in the center of a beautiful, fragrant rose of white-yellow light with pink around the edges of its petals. It is the *Gloria Dei,*, the 'Glory of God' rose, with the white-golden flame burning in its center.

As you breathe in the soft fragrance and healing colors of this rose into your heart, the same pink diamond, rainbow laser beams of light continue to emanate out from the rose in your heart.

AFFIRM: "I AM INBREATHING AND ABSORBING GOD'S LOVE INTO EVERY CELL, ATOM, ORGAN, TISSUE AND MOLECULE OF MY BODY. I AM FILLED WITH THE HEALING ESSENCE OF GOD'S LOVE. I AM THE PRESENCE OF GOD'S LOVE IN ACTION HERE." (3x).

As you exhale, the whole room you are in is filled with the fragrance and light of this rose. As you bring your attention back to the rose in your heart the white-golden flame has transformed into a small ball of pink, white and yellow light. As you move closer to this ball of light you begin to recognize a small embryo that is surrounded by a mother of pearl aura. This embryo begins to unfold and move as you breathe, it begins to breathe with you. You are deeply moved to see that this embryo is your own inner child being birthed in unconditional love, nurturing, and total acceptance. You are now birthing your new Self, healing your inner child by giving it unconditional love and acceptance. The embryo in the center of the rose is now a little baby whose radiance envelops you with the purest love and innocence you have ever known. Embrace this inner child with all your heart, giving it a total welcome. Give it all the love you have. Now ask what this child wants from you.

Enfold your inner child in the pink diamond, rainbow laser beams of light you created earlier. Visualize the mother of pearl rainbow aura of the child open itself to receive your love. Your whole body and being is now merged with the soft, mother of pearl rainbow light with a pink aura all around it. Place the palms of your hands on your heart center and hold them there gently, in-breathing and exhaling slowly as you merge with these colors and your inner child. Allow the tender, loving qualities of the divine mother within you to embrace and nurture your inner child in unconditional love and accep-tance. Tell your inner child that you are always there for it and that you will never leave it. Allow this nurturing love deep into your heart, as you heal your own inner child. When you feel ready, slowly come back into physi-cal consciousness. Give yourself time to make this transi-tion smoothly as you prepare for the activation of the next light ray.

## THE COBALT BLUE RAY
CORRESPONDING ENERGY CENTER (CHAKRA): THROAT (See page 133)
PRESIDING MASTER: EL MORYA
ARCHANGEL: MICHAEL
ELOHIM: HERCULES
QUALITIES and FOCUS OF RAY: The Balanced use and physical manifestation of God's Will, Power, Initia-tion, Protection, Faith, Communication, Creative Expression and Projection into Form, and Leaderhip Ability.
CORRESPONDING GEMSTONE: TANZANITE, BLUE SAPPHIRE, BLUE DIAMOND, ROYAL BLUE TOUR-MALINE, LAPIS LAZULI, LAZULITE, APETITE, SIBERIAN BLUE QUARTZ with Cobalt.

The reason that the Blue Ray is known as the first ray is because the very first aspect of any creation is will and intention. Without will or directed intention, there is no movement or life. Divine Will empowers us with Life and Action, as we learn to develop our ability to manifest our goals, visions and desires into physical reality. Being able to communicate our ideas, feelings and thoughts by bringing them into physical expression is an aspect of the blue ray. All forms of leadership come under the radiation of the blue ray. Unfortunately there have been many leaders who have developed a very strong will (Hitler, Kruschev, Sadam Hussein, etc.) but have not learned how to direct that energy in balance with love and wisdom for the benefit of humanity. The blue ray assists in teaching us how to direct this power to benefit all life.

Another very important quality of the Blue Ray is faith. Without faith, there is no manifestation. As faith involves surrender, it teaches us to have a greater trust in our I AM Presence (Our True Self) and the universe. When you make your call to manifest something that you desire in life, be sure that you qualify that call with faith. Any doubts, especially self-doubts create gaps in your aura that block the full release of the desired manifestation. If you have difficulty in trusting yourself or the universe, or if you don't believe in yourself, it is probably a good idea to invoke the added assistance of the cobalt blue ray. This ray will also assist you to expand your powers of communication, creative expression, personal empowerment and to manifest your life purpose in this physical dimension.

### INVOKING and ACTIVATING
### the COBALT BLUE RAY
### GUIDED MEDITATION AND VISUALIZATION

Bring your attention to your throat center and start to visualize a radiant cobalt blue light radiating out from that center. Within that center of blue light is a pulsating crystal white light, and around that white light is a light blue radiance; as the blue expands outwardly, it becomes even deeper and more saturated in hue until it turns into a deep electric cobalt-royal blue. Breathe in this blue light into your throat center and as you exhale, exhale the crystal white light and let it fill your aura with its radiance. Continue inbreathing blue light into your throat and exhaling white light for about three minutes until you become filled with this blue and white light. There is now a clear crystal white light all around your whole body. The shining radiance of that white light as it extends outward merges with the light blue until it reaches a deeper, more electric cobalt blue light. Feel the penetrating coolness and power of this cobalt blue ray enfold and recharge all your cells, re-energizing and empowering your entire body and aura with vitality and strength.

AFFIRM: "I AM the Power and Projection of all the energy I require to manifest perfection in my being and world. My will is in full alignment with God's Will. I AM the Presence manifesting God's Will in all areas of my life. I AM filled and recharged with the Power, Strength, and Protection of my I AM Presence."

Visualize in front of you a beautiful snow-covered mountain-scape. It is nighttime, and there is a large, full golden moon shining above the high, snow-covered mountain peaks. You feel like you are in the Himalayas, near the crown of the world. As you look around you, you see the sky covered with millions of stars, and as you look further ahead of you, you notice a shimmering white-blue light hovering near the top of one of the highest mountain peaks in front of you. You also see the golden reflection of the moon on top of that snow-covered mountain. As you slowly begin to move towards that mountain, you discover a guide in the distance who will take you up this mountain. All around you is nothing but snow-covered mountains and brilliant sparks of diamond-like stars in the midnight sky. As you ascend up the mountain, you begin to hear beautiful celestial music that draws you even closer to the brilliant white-blue light up ahead of you.

As you continue climbing, your guide motions you to go up the white marble staircase that leads to this brilliant white-blue light in front of you. As you approach this dazzling light, you see an opening in the center of that light. You are now standing near the entrance of a beautiful, sparkling, white crystal temple. The guide next to you motions you to enter, and as you do, your whole body and being is re-energized in the essence of that brilliant white-blue light until you yourself become a blazing, transparent crystal of white-blue light.

As you step into this crystalline white temple, you see ahead of you a simple, crystal white altar in a golden archway. As you near this altar, you see a shining object of light on it. It too has the same white-blue radiance as your own aura. As you move closer to this radiant object, you realize that this is the source of the celestial music that you hear. You are now enfolded in this music, empowered by its Presence and radiance. You step even closer to the altar, wanting to touch this brilliant object. As you reach out to touch it, you recognize this shimmering object to be a beautiful crystal scepter whose top is a most dazzling, brilliant white-blue diamond sphere. Around the crystalline stem are tiny sparks of laser rainbow light beams; all around the white-blue diamond at the top are brilliant, more extended laser beams of the most beautiful, crystalline, rainbow spectrum radiating out in all directions from the center of the diamond.

As you pick up this sacred object of great power and light, you place it into your right hand, and touch it to your heart center. As you breathe in the radiant essence of this white-blue diamond and all its colors into your heart, you exhale the same tiny laser beams of rainbow light until your entire aura is filled with millions of sparkling rainbow laser beams of light. Now bring the scepter to your throat center and hold it there. Your Inner Voice becomes One with the Celestial Music. Your power of creative expression is now being unleashed, activated and energized. Your ability to communicate and speak your truth is also fully activated. You feel very much at ease in your own Power, as your own Identity is stabilized and integrated with your I AM Presence and your physical body. Your body, mind and spirit is now completely recharged and filled with the brilliant diamond essence of the Cobalt Blue Ray. Your ability and power to act in alignment with God's Will is now fully activated. You feel deep gratitude as you are enfolded and embraced in the Power and Majesty of your very own I AM GOD PRESENCE. As you reclaim your true power and identity, whenever you affirm "I AM", you will do so with greater conviction and empowerment that will make all your affirmations more powerful and effective. AFFIRM: "I AM THE PRESENCE AND POWER OF GOD'S WILL MANIFEST IN ALL MY THOUGHTS, FEELINGS AND ACTIONS."

As you reclaim your Power, you now have the ability to restructure your life into the perfection you desire. As you continue holding this powerful scepter, you can direct it to any part of your body or life that needs balancing and healing. During this process ask for your will to be in total alignment with God's Will as you learn to direct this cosmic beam of power, energy and strength wherever it is needed. As you hold this scepter, claim your own I AM God Dominion and ask that whatever energy has been misqualified or abused in your life, be totally restructured and replaced with the original blueprint of God's Divine Will and Perfection for your lifestream. As you begin to turn over your power and will to Divine Will, this process of surrender will assist you and guide you to make the necessary choices to manifest your life goals.

When you feel complete in your personal empowerment (whether it is toward a relationship, career, personal healing, etc.) gently put the crystal scepter back on the altar and affirm gratitude to your God Presence for this great gift of empowerment. **It is yours whenever you need it.**

## THE EMERALD-INDIGO RAY
CORRESPONDING ENERGY CENTER: THIRD EYE
(The center point above the eyebrows)
(See page 134)
PRESIDING MASTER: HILARION, MOTHER MARY
ARCHANGEL: RAPHAEL
ELOHIM: VISTA and CRYSTAL
QUALITIES AND FOCUS OF RAY: HEALING, Opening of the Third Eye, the ability to FOCUS through creative visualization and holding a one-pointed focus, PRECIPITATION, CONSECRATION, PROSPERITY, CLAIRVOYANCE and CLAIRAUDIENCE. All forms of Extra Sensory Perception.

CORRESPONDING GEMSTONE: EMERALD, TOURMA-
LINE, AVENTURINE, PERIDOT, DEMANTOID,
GREEN GOSSULAR, GREEN ZOISITE, MAL-
ACHITE, MOLDAVITE, DIOPSIDE, CHRYSO-
PRASE, VERDELITE, ALEXENDRITE, GREEN
FLOURITE, DIOPTASE, SODALITE, SUGILITE.

In any process of creation, manifestation or healing,
there must first be a VISION together with the intention
guiding the desired manifestation into form. One of the
primary qualities of the Emerald-Indigo Ray is to open
and expand our Inner Vision (Third Eye), our Inner
Hearing, and our Intuition (Inner Feeling), so we can
develop higher levels of interdimensional communication with higher forms of life and intelligence in the
universe. Through the power of one-pointed concentration and focus, we gradually learn to develop these extra-
sensory powers of our intuitive awareness to a more
refined and perfected degree. This naturally requires
some determination, self-discipline, practice, commitment and meditation to achieve effective results. As you
develop an inner peace and stillness through your meditations, you will gradually begin to distill outer, mun-
dane distractions.

When you are in a deep state of meditative inner
peace, your entire body becomes a finely tuned instrument that facilitates the expansion and opening of your
third eye. As this light within you starts to build in
frequency, you will be able to channel this light energy
into any area of your body or life that needs healing or
creative manifestation. Learning to focus that light within
your inner third eye in a one-pointed way allows you
to precipitate and manifest through the power of creative visualization as you hold and energize this vision

in your third eye. Your power to physically manifest what you want in life becomes more effective when you hold this Vision in Light, and allow it to be consecrated. **Consecration** means to make sacred, or the 'act of blessing'. Before any healing or creation can fully manifest, it goes through several stages of clearing and adjustment according to the quality of your will, clarity of purpose, love energy, faith, purity and vision. As your intention and purpose become more clear and you make the call to your I AM Presence, higher ascended beings of light, as well as your own God-Self, are there to assist you in manifesting your vision through their unified energies as they CONSECRATE and hold that vision in the Light. Once the Vision is consecrated, it is ready to come into physical manifestation. Your powers of creative visualization and manifestation are as strong as your feeling world. As you qualify your Vision or goal with more love, light, and FEELING, the stronger and more effective will be your manifestation. Calling on the Archangel Raphael greatly assists this process of consecration, precipitation, and healing. **The Emerald-Green Ray is also the primary ray for HEALING, ABUNDANCE and PROSPERITY.**

Utilize this light ray wisely so it benefits all life around you, as you learn to consecrate the energy and abundance that comes into your life with love and gratitude for what you DO have. This opens the door for unlimited abundance and prosperity to manifest in your life. A wonderful way to do this is to bless all the money that comes into your hands and use, with the love and light of Christ and your I AM God Presence. As you bless this money and send it back into the world, visualize this blessing and goodwill touching the person receiving this money. This will also assist them in creating more abundance, prosperity and good health. A very wonderful and effective **affirmation** for this is: **"Thank you God, for all the abundance that comes into my life** as a free gift of your love.   I AM THE PRESENCE BLESSING AND CONSE-CRATING THIS MONEY WITH THE LOVE AND LIGHT OF GOD, SO THAT WHEREVER IT GOES IT BRINGS RADIANT HEALTH, ILLUMINATION, LOVE AND UNLIMITED ABUN-DANCE TO THE PERSON RECEIVING IT. MANIFEST. MANI-FEST. MANIFEST. THANK YOU. BELOVED I AM. BELOVED I AM. BELOVED I AM."


## THE EMERALD-INDIGO RAY
### GUIDED MEDITATION and VISUALIZATION

As you go deeper within your sacred inner chamber, visualize a spiral of emerald green light encircling your body starting from your feet and legs and moving all the way up to enfold your crown; then it returns back down again until this emerald light surrounds the foundation of where you are sitting. Absorb this spiralling action of the Emerald Green Healing Ray into your body.  Feel its comforting, soothing coolness enfold your entire being with a calm and serenity that makes your whole body relaxed and receptive to these soothing emerald rays of healing.

As you inbreathe, start breathing in this emerald green light into your lungs, visualizing this healing green light entering all your cells, oxygenating all your cells with the healing life force of the green  ray. All your cells are beginning to absorb this green ray. When you exhale, breathe out a concentration of this green light and let it fill your aura with the Emerald Green Ray of Healing. As you continue inbreathing this emerald light, hold your breath for a few seconds and feel the cells in your lungs ABSORB this healing green as all your blood cells are being fed with this nurturing and life-supportive light ray. You are now totally surrounded in the cosmic Emerald-Indigo Ray of Healing.

There are around you and above you celestial light beings who are the guardians of this Light Ray. They stand in their radiant Light Bodies, ready to assist you in your next step of unfolding into the Healing Presence of your very own Radiant God Self. Invoke the Presence of your own I AM God-Self from within your heart center. Call upon all the angelic beings, Presences and Masters of Consecration and Healing to enfold you and your I AM God Presence in their radiant love essence. You may call upon **Mother Mary, Master Hilarion, Archangel Raphael, and the Elohim Vista and Crystal** to assist you in consecrating all your energies in order to help you manifest something that you wish to bring into form. This can be in the form of a personal healing, creating abundance, a loving relationship, or a creative artistic project.

As you align your will with your I AM Presence and the Celestial Guardians surrounding you, you begin to let go of all effort and desire to control or manipulate the energy within and around you. Simply allow the love and light within you to merge into a surrendered space of Grace. Feel every particle of energy around your body scintillate with sparkles of rainbow-white light energy, clearing your entire aura with a new brilliant radiance that showers you with waves upon waves of blessings as your energy field is being cleared. As you learn to let go and allow the Presence within you to guide you, you are opening another door to your empowerment. As your I AM GOD PRESENCE is merging with all of the radiant

Celestial Guardians of the Emerald Indigo Ray of Healing, a new, open doorway filled with radiant light appears in front of you. As you move toward this open doorway, you see a blazing white light in its center, surrounded by a golden yellow, and a radiant deep emerald green light. This light is welcoming you, as you approach the open door of light.

As you step through the threshold of the doorway and into the light, you feel completely safe and comfortable. Your whole body feels energized and renewed. All your fears are dissolving as you are surrounded by the gentle warmth of a tender, loving PRESENCE. In front of you is a beautiful white throne that sits on top of an emerald stairway. On each side of the empty throne is a radiant angelic Presence welcoming you. To the left of you stands the beloved Elohim Vista and to the right the Elohim Crystal. Both angelic forms are radiant essences of transluscent, white rainbow light weaving through their transparent light bodies. Their soft smiles welcome you as they motion you to come up the stairway and for you to take your seat on the white throne.

As you reach the top platform and face the throne, the radiant Presence of Master Hilarion appears behind the throne, his hands reaching out to welcome you as he motions you to take your seat. As you sit on the throne, a powerful, brilliant pyramid of emerald green light surrounds you. At the top apex of the pyramid stands the centralized focus of Master Hilarion and the other two points of light forming the base of the pyramid are the focal points of the Elohim Vista and Crystal. Standing in front of you is the Radiant Presence of Archangel Raphael, who holds a crystal scepter in his left hand. His right hand is extended palm-open facing you, blessing you with a brilliant light beam of the Emerald Green Healing Ray. He says to you that anytime you need his assistance especially in a healing process, a creative work, or just wish to help someone, to call on him and he will be present to assist you. As Archangel Raphael steps forward toward where you are sitting, he presents the crystal scepter to you. As you take the scepter into your right hand, you notice that the top of the scepter is made out of a brilliant pyramid-shaped emerald that sparkles like a green diamond. Inside the pyramid is a white-golden star that pulsates with the rhythm of your breathing. As you tune into this bright star, it has a message for you: "KNOW THAT THE HEALING PRESENCE AND POWER OF THE UNIVERSE COMES FROM THE HEART OF GOD AND THAT THIS SAME HEALING PRESENCE AND POWER IS WITHIN YOUR OWN HEART. ALWAYS MAKE YOUR CALL FROM WITHIN YOUR HEART, AND ASK THAT THE HEALING POWER AND LIGHT OF YOUR GREAT I AM PRESENCE DIRECT THIS LIGHT TO WHEREVER IT IS NEEDED IN YOUR BODY OR BEING. I will now give you one of the most powerful and sacred AFFIRMATIONS to assist you in any healing process. Use it often whenever you need: **AFFIRM: "I AM THE HEALING PRESENCE AND POWER OF GOD'S INFINITE LOVE AND LIGHT."**

As you hear this affirmation and repeat it yourself, the power and grace of your acceptance flows through your whole body. The scepter you are holding is a sacred tool of your empowerment, of your I AM Presence. It is your gift to accept this empowerment and to use it wisely for the benefit of all life and humanity. As you hold the crystal scepter to your heart center, the beloved Elohim Crystal stands in front of you. In her right hand she holds a brilliant, white diamond the size and shape of an eye.

As she lifts this diamond teardrop, she places it directly above your eyebrows in the middle of your forehead and says to you: "As I implant this diamond crystal into your third eye, you will be able to access infinite dimensions of light through the power of one-pointed focus and concentration. Use this power and energy wisely to assist humanity and the life around you for healing, as you learn to precipitate into physical form the perfection with whom you are becoming One. Your powers of inner perception will now expand to consecrate your One-Pointed-Vision by holding it in the Light, with the crystalline substance of God-Purity, creating an accelerated momentum of Light that will set life free within you and around you." Your entire focus and attention is now amplified and expanded, as the concentrated light energy within your third eye is activated. Beams of radiant white, rainbow light energy pour out of your awareness, as you journey into new dimensions of light.

When you feel ready, slowly come back into your physical body by taking a few slow deep breaths.

## THE GOLDEN-YELLOW RAY

**CORRESPONDING ENERGY CENTER:** TOP OF THE HEAD, CROWN AREA. (See page 135)
**PRESIDING MASTER:** KUTHUMI
**ARCHANGEL:** JOPHIEL
**ELOHIM:** CASSIOPIA
**QUALITIES AND FOCUS OF RAY:** WISDOM, DISCERNMENT, ILLUMINATION and ENLIGHTENMENT. Understanding the Laws of Universal Creation.
**CORRESPONDING GEMSTONE:** GOLDEN CITRINE,

## TOPAZ, YELLOW DIAMOND, APATITE, SPINEL, HELIODOR, GOLDEN BERYL, YELLOW SAPPHIRE, CHRYSOBERYL, NOBLE ORTHOCLASE

One of the most important qualities of the Golden Ray is the ability to understand and utilize the universal laws of creation. This process involves **developing our discernment, by fine-tuning our perceptions and learning to distinguish between the projections of Illusion and True Higher Reality.** As your ability to focus and fine-tune your awareness through the process of discernment increases, more universal intelligence will manifest in your daily reality. This intelligence will guide you to make clearer and more positive choices that will help you to manifest greater perfection, harmony and love into your life.

WISDOM IS PURE CONSCIOUSNESS IN ACTION. The Golden Ray is the emanation and living manifestation of Universal Love merged with the **full awareness of Itself** in harmony with all life and creation. This universal intelligence dissolves the veils and illusions of duality, enlightening and healing the separation that is caused through ignorance and identification with the mind. PURE CONSCIOUSNESS IS A STATE OF ONE-NESS FREE FROM THE ILLUSION AND CONDITIONED PROJECTION OF DUALITY.

When we recognize that the true nature of our Self is non-dual, we begin to heal the projected illusions of duality within our mind. Since there is only One Self, this realization sets us free as we move beyond the projections of the mind. As long as the mind continues to act and react out of fear, it will continue to spin the wheel of illusion and propel our feelings and emotions into a treadmill of helplessness and suffering.

Enlightenment is the awakening of universal love (with our Self) and **consciously** directing this love energy into all areas of our Being, until full awareness of SELF is realized through the balanced use and mastery of Divine Will and Love in Action. As we develop greater self-love and understanding of life's purpose in relation to our human and spiritual development, we Become the Enlightenment we seek.

### ACTIVATING and INVOKING
### THE GOLDEN YELLOW RAY
### GUIDED MEDITATION and VISUALIZATION

Begin by taking several slow deep breaths in and out. Start inbreathing golden light into your heart center. As you exhale, breathe out this golden-white light all around your head and crown. Visualize this golden light enfolding your entire head and crown area with its glowing radiance. Do this breathing and visualization for about two-three minutes.

Now, as you inbreathe, breathe in the golden light into your crown and head. Feel your head surrounded and illuminated in this warm golden glow. As you exhale, release this golden light all around your body. Feel your aura being filled with this shimmering, irridescent, golden light. After inbreathing golden light into your crown, hold your breath a few seconds and add a touch of white light to the golden light. As you exhale, begin filling your aura with a shimmering golden-white radiance. Your entire being is shimmering in this golden-white radiance. You begin to see in the distance in front of you a transluscent, crystalline, white-golden ball of light. As that ball of light comes closer to you, the form begins to move, and as the form gets closer, it starts to unfold into a magnificent temple of crystal white light with an irridescent golden aura surrounding it. In front of the temple is an open entry, filled with radiant golden light. There is a tall staircase that leads to this entrance, and your focus is on the golden light of this open door. Slowly you begin to mount the many steps that lead to the open portal of light. As you near the entrance, you see in front of you a radiant Being of Light that is so brilliant you cannot distinguish its form or features. As you pause in the entrance, your entire being is magnetically charged with the same radiant light essence as the shimmering Being in front of you. There are spirals of irridescent golden-white light all around your body, spiralling faster and faster all around you, transforming your entire physical body into living electrons of liquid golden-white light, until your entire body becomes a transparent body of shimmering light.

You feel a powerful, permeating Presence of Love all around you, as well as within you. You realize that the same brilliant golden white light and love energy that is around you is also within you now. You feel safe now to go inside the temple. As you move closer to the radiant light being in front of you, you begin to recognize that this beautiful being is wearing a golden, crystalline crown of radiant jewels. Each gem is glowing and sparkling with the light rays of the rainbow. As you look into the eyes and the face of this radiant being, you begin to recognize this beautiful Being as your very own radiant God-Self.

As your Golden I AM Presence extends their arms to embrace and welcome you, you slowly open your own arms as you move closer to embrace each other. As you embrace, the golden-white liquid light of your I AM God Presence is interpenetrating with your luminous light body, filling it with a new crystalline substance and life energy you have not felt before. As you merge with your golden 'I AM PRESENCE', your body takes on all the shimmering irridescent colors of the rainbow. Feel the Presence and Power of Universal Love and Intelligence expand within your heart and crown as you are reunited with your True Self.

As you step back and open your eyes, you see that the radiant Light Being in front of you has dissolved and dematerialized. In front of you now is a tall, beautiful crystal-framed mirror, and as you look into that mirror, you see the same radiant Light Being that you first saw in the open doorway. As your hands move up toward your head, you realize that there is a golden crown on top of it. It is the very same crystalline crown that you saw on the Being in front of you earlier. As you step closer to the mirror, you recognize that it is your True Self that you are looking at. Tears of gratitude and joy fill your heart as you see your new radiant, True Self reflected in the mirror in front of you.

As you recognize your own crystalline reflection, you realize that you and your radiant I AM God Presence have completely merged into One Being, One Body, One Mind, and One Heart. This realization brings you great joy and exhilaration as you feel completely empowered and recharged with the elixir of eternal light and life. As you step closer to the mirror, you reach out to touch it, but there is nothing to touch. It is all an etheric substance of light energy. An inner voice guides you to step through the mirror. As you do so, you realize that the mirror is yet another interdimensional doorway to your Self. As you step through the mirror, you pass through a softly-lit tunnel of warm golden-yellow light. At the end of the tunnel is a sky blue light, and as you step out of the tunnel into the blue light, you slowly come back into your physical body where you are now sitting.

Continue breathing slowly and deeply as you integrate the interdimensional experience you just had. You may want to ask your I AM PRESENCE and the Masters on the Golden Ray to assist you in anchoring this Light Ray into your physical reality.

AFFIRM: "Beloved Mighty I AM PRESENCE, Beloved Master KUTHUMI, Archangel JOPHIEL, and Beloved Elohim CASSIOPIA: Please anchor within my physical, mental, emotional, and etheric body the PRESENCE, qualities, and benefits of the Golden Ray of Illumination. Expand my capacity for understanding and mastering the laws of creation and universal intelligence. Guide me to perfect my discernment so that I can make all my choices in clarity and wisdom. I AM now enfolded in the electronic light substance of the Golden Ray. **I AM GOD-ILLUMINATION. I AM GOD-WISDOM. I AM THE ENLIGHT-ENMENT WITHIN THE HEART AND MIND OF GOD.** I consciously accept this now. Manifest. Manifest. Manifest. BELOVED I AM" (3x).

## THE MOTHER OF PEARL RAY
CORRESPONDING ENERGY CENTER:   ABOVE YOUR CROWN, The Opening of the Silver Cord. (Antakharana) (See page 136)

PRESIDING MASTER:    MOTHER MARY, AEOLUS,
MAHA-CHOHAN, LORD MAITREYA, YOUR I
AM GOD PRESENCE, YOUR TWIN-FLAME, AND
YOUR CHRIST-SELF.
QUALITIES AND FOCUS OF RAY:  The INTEGRATION of
All the Eight Universal Light Rays. The full activation
of the Soul plane of Consciousness . REUNION with
YOUR ESSENCE-TWIN or TWIN-FLAME.
CORRESPONDING GEMSTONE: MOTHER OF PEARL,
PUREST, CLEAREST QUARTZ CRYSTAL WITH
RAINBOW INCLUSIONS, SELENITE.

Within the Mother of Pearl Ray is the activation and
full awareness of the soul plane of consiousness. This includes your transpersonal communion with Ascended
Masters, Angelic Presences, Guides, and other Light
Beings who are working with you to assist you in fulfilling your life purpose here on earth.  The Mother of Pearl
Ray also contains the full integration of all the seven
cosmic light rays as they are fully activated. These become the rainbow bridge of light between your human
and Divine Self. Add a touch of white light to this rainbow light and you have an irridescent Mother of Pearl
rainbow.

When all of the seven Light Rays have merged and are
in balance within you, you experience a profound transformation of the entire atomic structure of your being.
This includes major shifts in your physical, mental,
emotional, and etheric body.  As all four bodies are
harmonized and balanced within the integration of all
the Light Rays, your body and being becomes fully
aligned with your soul-purpose, assisting you to activate
and fulfill your life goals as you achieve mastery on earth.

Another aspect of your soul activation is the pulsating magnetic attraction of your Essence-Twin also known as your Twin-Flame which is the other half of your Self. Seventy-five percent of the time, your other half is not in physical embodiment, but lives in a more spiritual light dimension. You can meet your Twin-Flame on the inner planes or you can even meet them on earth; however, this is a rare occurence and happens only about twenty-five percent of the time when both twin flames incarnate on earth at the same time. As you approach the completion of your mastery on earth and prepare for your Ascension, you will once more meet and be reunited with this vital part of your Self.

As your soul purpose becomes fully activated within the cellular and atomic pattern of your body, you will begin to utilize these sacred tools (The Eight Universal Light Rays) and apply them in your daily life for your healing, transformation and mastery. One key to this mastery is your ability to integrate and bring into balance and alignment both your interpersonal identity as well as your transpersonal I AM PRESENCE.

## THE MOTHER OF PEARL RAY
**Anchoring your Light Body into Physical Reality**
GUIDED MEDITATION AND VISUALIZATION

As you have now absorbed and activated all the Seven Light Rays into your aura, you are now ready to anchor and integrate the soul activation of your Light Body into Physical Reality. Visualize a soft milky-white rainbow aura of irridescent light all around you. All your seven energy centers (chakras) are in perfect alignment and harmony with one another. There is an open, free flow of energy between the base of your spine and your crown center.

As you breathe in and out, visualize the mother of pearl colors and light entering your body as you in-breathe, and as you exhale, your aura fills with the softness of the rainbow white light. Bathe in the softness and gentleness of the irridescent mother of pearl light essence. Your whole body and being rejoices in the visu-alizations and affirmations that you have invoked for your mastery and healing. Every cell, atom and organ of your body rejoices as it receives this input of love and light energy. **You have activated the light of your soul as it pours into every cell, atom and organ of your physical body, anchoring, grounding and stabilizing that Light within and around you.** You have created a powerful magnetic energy field and resonance of electronic light and illumination that is permanently being anchored within the cellular network of your body.

Your whole being is emanating gratitude and joy for the unlimited expression of love and light you are giving to your Self. Your I AM GOD PRESENCE rejoices in your acknowledgment of your very own true SELF. As a glad free gift from your own Source of Light and Empower-ment, your Radiant I AM GOD PRESENCE is now standing in front of you. This being is a beautiful, attractive, radiant woman or man dressed in a white irridescent mother-of pearl robe with a golden sash around the waist. The aura around this being is also an irridescent mother of pearl rainbow white light, with diamond-like sparks radiating out from the aura creating a gorgeous brilliant aureole of light all around you. This man or woman is the person and lover of your dreams. Everything that you have ever wanted your intimate lover to be is standing right in front of you with open arms outstretched, inviting you into their open arms. Your feel a rose-colored light open your heart center as you are automatically magnetized to this being. As you stand up and walk towards your Essence-Twin, a shimmering radiant beam of Light from both your hearts flow into one anothers' heart centers.

As you both stand facing each other, a laser beam of indigo and emerald crystal light from your third eye merges through the laser beam into your Twin-Flame's third eye. Gradually you notice that each of your chakras are sending out a radiant beam of light connecting each others' energy centers through the multi-colored rainbow light beams.

As your energies merge, the pleasure and ecstacy you feel and experience in each center within your body is beyond description. You feel completely In-Love with one another as all your energy centers are merging, uniting in one orgasmic cosmic breath of Rainbow Light. Your open energy centers are now simultaneously receiving and transmitting this rainbow light energy.

As the two of you embrace, all veils of separation are lifted and dissolved forever. As you merge into your Twin-Flame, both your Light Bodies become ONE BRIL-LIANT FLAME OF LIGHT. You feel tremendously empowered as you release all concepts of Self and identity. **This merging and REUNION is your Initiation into wholeness and One-ness with your own Christ-Essence and your Essence-Twin.**

As you stand UNITED, you reach out your arms with open palms to receive the BENEDICTION and CONSECRATION of your ASCENSION as you are completely merged with your Twin Flame and your Beloved I AM GOD PRESENCE.


**AFFIRM:**
**"I AM THE RESURRECTION, THE LIFE, AND THE PERFECTION OF MY ETERNAL GOD-PRESENCE FULLY AND PHYSICALLY MANIFEST HERE ON EARTH NOW. I AM THE FULL ACCEPTANCE AND FULL USE OF ALL THE POWERS OF THE BEING THAT I AM."**

I AM THE LIGHT OF GOD THAT NEVER FAILS.
I AM THE ASCENSION IN THE LIGHT.

BELOVED I AM, BELOVED I AM, BELOVED I  AM."

∞

# 25

# THE NEW HEALING COLORS
## THE THERAPEUTIC APPLICATIONS OF
## COLOR-LIGHT AND
## CORRESPONDING GEMSTONES*

### WHITE

White is the color of purity, unity, and harmony. It signifies the transpersonal and universal Light of God and creation. White light is a universal color, as it automatically restores balance to any part of our body that is out of alignment, or needs healing. Since it contains all the colors of the rainbow spectrum, the body will automatically absorb whatever color it needs for healing itself. White is also the color of essence and simplicity and has the greatest dynamic range to **expand** our consciousness and aura. White light balances our seven energy centers, especially the pineal and pituitary gland. White is also the universal color of Integration and Harmony.

\* For a color chart illustrating the following colors, please see Color Plate 3.

CORRESPONDING GEMSTONES: WHITE DIAMOND, QUARTZ CRYSTAL, SELENITE, ULEXITE, DANBURITE, WHITE TOPAZ, WHITE ZIRCON, WHITE SAPPHIRE.
THERAPEUTIC APPLICATIONS: Helps expand spiritual awareness. Restores balance and harmony to all seven energy centers (chakras). Universal color for Spiritual Healing and Protection.

## MOTHER OF PEARL

All pearlescent colors come under this category. (See Color Plate 4 ) This includes soft pastel hues with a slight irridescence to them. The Mother of Pearl essence has a very high vibration. Since it contains all the rainbow colors mixed with white light, it has great therapeutic value. Its soothing, calming quality nurtures and softens our energy, as it re-balances and re-integrates the energy flow of our emotional and feeling body.

The Mother of Pearl is the feminine aspect of divine love that enhances our aura with a purity that allows us to be more open and receptive to love. It stimulates the nurturing and caring, devotional aspect of our Self. Since this color frequency has predominant colors of pink, turquoise and violet, it is an excellent color for healing emotional wounds, since it contains the quality of transmutation (violet), love (pink), and communication (turquoise). The Mother of Pearl is also an effective integrator of our emotional, mental, physical and etheric bodies. It is most effective in harmonizing our aura and re-balancing our emotional energy field. It is the perfect color frequency to work with when we wish to anchor and expand the receptive, nurturing, feminine aspect of love. It also activates our soul memory, as it contains the integration of all seven rays.

CORRESPONDING GEMSTONES: MOTHER OF PEARL, MILKY WHITE OPAL WITH RAINBOW COLORS.
THERAPEUTIC APPLICATIONS: Soothes and nurtures our nerves and emotional body. Stabilizes and expands our receptive, loving, nurturing feminine aspect. Integrates the mental, emotional, physical and etheric bodies. Activates soul memory.

## IRRIDESCENT ABALONE COLORS
### THE BRIGHTER, MORE ELECTRIC RAINBOW HUES

The colors found in most abalone shells have a very bright irridescense of violet, turquoise, blue, and pink. (See Color Plate 4 ) The colors within this spectrum have a very similar effect in energizing, harmonizing, and clearing the aura as the Mother of Pearl, except the effect is more pronounced and more concentrated in intensity. Wearing these bright abalone colors brings in a higher vibration of light and energy into the aura. If we need more vitality and energy, and want to harmonize the emotions with the physical body, these colors are an excellent choice. These colors also stimulate and activate the light frequency of our I AM Presence and the Eight Light Rays.

CORRESPONDING GEMSTONES: ABALONE SEA SHELL, FIRE OPAL, LABRADORITE.
THERAPEUTIC APPLICATIONS: Restores energy, balance and vitality to our physical, mental and emotional body. Activates our etheric body. It is very healing to gaze into a beautiful abalone seashell and absorb its therapeutic color frequencies. It is also the color spectrum for energizing and integrating all the chakras.

## INDIGO

The color indigo is a very powerful, high-energy, light vibration that activates and expands our psychic abilities (third eye) such as E.S.P., clairvoyance, clairaudience and intuitive awareness. It stimulates the opening of the pineal gland which expands our capacity for creative visualization and manifestation. Many souls presently incarnating on earth have a predominance of this indigo light frequency in their aura as they bring these more highly developed powers of telepathy and interdimensional awareness into the earth plane. Indigo helps us to see into our subconscious and to penetrate deeper into the causal plane. This insight opens new levels of communication and perception, as the invisible is gradually revealed and developed through our Inner Vision, and becomes a living, tangible Reality for our transformation and healing.

CORRESPONDING GEMSTONES: DEEP SUGILITE, AZURITE, SODALITE, DEEP TANZANITE, SOME CHINESE FLOURITE.
THERAPEUTIC APPLICATIONS: Excellent nerve tonic. Improves eyesight, good for over-active thyroid, tones muscles, soothes our energy, helps to balance emotional body.

## VIOLET

Violet is the color ray for TRANSMUTATION AND ACCELERATION. Since this color is the fastest vibrating color of the rainbow spectrum, it has the greatest capacity to cut through blocked energies, or accumulation of negative energy in our mental, emotional, physical and etheric bodies. It has the power to dissolve and transmute dense energies into a more refined and perfected state. It is a powerful color that helps dissolve self-abusive, destructive mental and emotional patterns that have become crystallized in the etheric (causal) body. Violet automatically raises the vibratory energy of the person working with this color and light. Wearing the corresponding gemstones (especially Amethyst and Sugilite) amplifies the activity of the violet ray. Violet is also the color representing all New Age Enterprises, businesses, and alternative energy networks that are supporting and expanding the life essence upon planet earth.

**CORRESPONDING GEMSTONES:** AMETHYST, SUGULITE, VIOLET SAPPHIRE, FLOURITE.
**THERAPEUTIC APPLICATIONS:** Calming effect on nerves, helps dissolve addictions, good for kidneys, promotes bone growth, good for over active heart palpitations and rheumatism.

## COBALT–ROYAL BLUE

This is the color for confidence, power, and will. It is a perfect color to utilize and wear for those who need more initiative, self-assurance, protection, and the ability to communicate and project your ideas to the public. If you suffer from low self-esteem and don't feel that you are in your own power, the cobalt blue is an excellent color choice. It will help you to stabilize your confidence and faith in yourself in order to reclaim your own personal power and identity. Blue is also the color of leadership, spiritual will and protection.

**CORRESPONDING GEMSTONES:** TANZANITE, ROYAL BLUE SAPPHIRE, LAPIS LAZULI, BLUE APETITE, LAZULITE, DEEP-

BLUE DIAMOND, ROYAL-BLUE TOURMALINE (Brazil), SIBE-RIAN BLUE QUARTZ INJECTED WITH COBALT.
THERAPEUTIC APPLICATIONS: Helps insomnia, soothes nerves, neutralizes inflammation, raises blood-pressure, also good for over-active heart palpitations, nausea, and recovery from shock.

## TURQUOISE
This is a great color for enhancing communication and personal creative expression. It helps to ground and integrate our intention-will (blue) with the expansion of the mind (yellow) which results in a more creative communication and expression. It also contains the healing energy of the green ray which helps us to focus our intention and vision toward a specific area of creative manifestation.

CORRESPONDING GEMSTONES: TURQUOISE, AMAZONITE, GEM-SILICA, AQUAMARINE, INDICOLITE, CHRYSOCOLLA, TURQUOISE COLORED TOURMALINE, HEMIMORPHITE, SMITHSONITE.

THERAPEUTIC APPLICATIONS: Excellent color for healthy skin tone, helps with the formation of new skin cells, soothing for an over active mind.

## EMERALD GREEN AND BLUE-GREEN
Emerald Green is one of the most effective color light frequencies to employ in any form of healing. Since it is neither too warm nor too cold in vibration, it has a mid-range frequency that is very healing and stabilizing for

the body. Green light and color is life supporting and nurturing to our physical health and growth. Emerald green is also effective (interchangeable with Indigo) in opening our inner eye (third eye), as it activates the pineal gland. Green is also the color of abundance, prosperity and nature.

**CORRESPONDING GEMSTONES:** EMERALD, TOURMALINE, AVENTURINE, PERIDOT, DEMANTOID, GREEN GROSSULAR, GREEN SAPPHIRE, GREEN ZOISITE, MALACHITE, MOLDAVITE, DIOPSIDE, CHRYSOPRASE, VERDELITE, ALEXANDRITE, GREEN FLOURITE, JADE, DIOPTASE.

**THERAPEUTIC APPLICATIONS:** One of the most healing colors of the light spectrum. Helps lower blood pressure, balances emotions, helps form healthy bones, muscles and tissue. Is a good sedative and has a calming effect. It is the color of vitality and growth.


## GOLDEN YELLOW

This color frequency contains the energizing solar rays which have a quality of warmth, cheerfulness, and joy. It is the most effective color for working on the mental plane, or expanding our intelligence and understanding of life and universal intelligence. Yellow helps us to concentrate and develop our mental capacities of perception and understanding. At the same time it has an uplifting, yet calming effect on our body and mind. A wide range color hue from pastel to brilliant irridescent, golden-yellow color is available to us in varying degrees and intensities in order to serve our individual needs. The frequency of golden-yellow color associated with the Ascended Masters is a glowing, irridescent gold and is an excellent color for accessing higher consciousness. Since this color is also a form of solar energy, it has the capacity to revitalize, enhance and expand our aura and our mental, emotional nature. Yellow is the color of EXPAN-SION.

**CORRESPONDING GEMSTONES:** GOLDEN CITRINE, TOPAZ, YELLOW DIAMOND, HELIODOR, GOLDEN BERYL, YELLOW SAPPHIRE, NOBLE ORTHOCLASE, SPINEL, CHRYSOBERYL.
**THERAPEUTIC APPLICATIONS:** Assists digestive system, good for liver, depression, purifies bloodstream, activates lymphatic system, strengthens nerves and brain.

## PASTEL YELLOW

This color has basically the same qualities and essence as Golden-Yellow except it contains more white light. It has a softer, gentler effect on the body and mind. There are times when it is very appropriate to wear softer pastel colors if we need a more soothing, calming energy, yet also wish to have the healing properties of the brighter colors in our aura. Since the pastel colors contain a more prominent degree of white light, the aura is able to select the exact intensity of color vibration it needs to absorb from within the white light spectrum of that pastel color. These soft, gentle colors are very balancing to our nerves, bringing increased light essence into our being and expanding our capacity to be more receptive and open. All pastel colors EXPAND our auric field, while darker colors (especially those containing black) CONTRACT the aura.

**CORRESPONDING GEMSTONES:** PALE CITRINE QUARTZ, PALE YELLOW SAPPHIRE, PALE CALCITE.

**THERAPEUTIC APPLICATIONS:** Same as golden-yellow except the effect is softer and milder.

## PASTEL PEACH-APRICOT

This is a great color for integrating both the physical and spiritual aspects of life. Since orange is energizing, and pink is the open energy of love, it is an effective combination when one's intention is to harmonize the physical and the spiritual planes. This color is also the color of spiritual devotion.

**CORRESPONDING GEMSTONES:** CORAL, PEACH-COLORED MORGANITE, CARNELIAN, TOPAZ, PEACH-COLORED OPAL, CALCITE, RHODONITE.
**THERAPEUTIC APPLICATIONS:** Good for gall bladder, kidney stones, stimulates thyroid gland, good for lungs.

## ROSE–PINK

This is the color of Love and represents the heart center. Needless to say, it has a very soothing effect and helps open our heart center. Pink also vibrates the loving qualities of compassion, mercy and forgiveness. For men or women who need more of these feminine qualities and balance in their lives, this is a perfect color to wear, such as shirts or sweaters, as well as to wear the corresponding gemstones such as kunzite and rose quartz. Wearing the rose-pink color will enhance the vibration of love within us. Pink is the color to visualize and wear when we wish to expand and express universal love energy in our life. It is also a very healing color when interchanged with emerald green (tourmaline). This helps to soothe and heal any contraction within the heart center. When pink is worn on the body, it magnetizes more love energy into your aura.

**CORRESPONDING GEMSTONES:** KUNZITE, ROSE QUARTZ, PINK OR WATERMELON TOURMALINE, MORGANITE, PINK TOPAZ, PINK SAPPHIRE, PINK DIAMOND, RHODOCROCITE, LAPIDOLITE, RHODONITE.

**THERAPEUTIC APPLICATIONS:** Enhances and expands our capacity to receive and express Love. Helps anemia, depression, good for low blood pressure.

## LAVENDER

This color has a very high vibration as you can see from the circular color patch. (See Color Plate 3) It contains a combination of Pink (Heart) and Blue (Willpower-Throat Center). It helps us to manifest divine love through the empowerment of our will. It gives direction to our love energy, as it is channeled into physical manifestation through creative expression in form. It is an excellent color to use in expanding love and creative expression in all human relationships. Lavender also expands our capacity for self-love, and strengthens our will to surrender more to the energy of love. It is a very harmonizing color vibration in the home. Worn on the upper part of the body, it enhances the love energy to flow more into the throat, heart and chest area. Lavender is a most effective color in externalizing your love energy as you direct your love toward a particular form of physical expression.

**CORRESPONDING GEMSTONES:** KUNZITE, LAVENDER JADE, LAVENDER AMETHYST, LAVENDER ROSE QUARTZ (Madagascar), LAVENDER SAPPHIRE, SMITHSONITE.
**THERAPEUTIC APPLICATIONS:** Integrates Love and Will by giving the Love Energy direction and form. Helps depression, has simultaneously both a soothing, calming, and uplifting vibrational effect.

# 26

# INTRODUCTION TO COLOR THERAPY
## DISPELLING THE ILLUSION
## OF GENDER IN COLOR THERAPY

One of the first points that need clarification when engaging in the therapeutic application and use of color is to dispell the illusion that certain colors are feminine and others masculine. For example, the color blue (baby clothes) is usually associated with male energy while pink is always associated with the feminine. During our present cultural and social development, both sexes need a tremendous re-balancing in their own feminine–masculine polarities.

Within every human being, both aspects need to be in harmony and balance with one another. Men are learning to express their feelings and emotions (Pink Ray), as well as developing their intuition (an associated female quality), while women are learning to "GO FOR IT!" and take charge of their lives (an associated male aspect) by becoming stronger and more assertive in their will–intention aspect (Blue Ray). One can see the importance of re-balancing these polarities, as the pendulum has swung to extreme poles, due to the repression and extremes of dysfunctional, limited, gender-role playing for the past few thousand years.

Unfortunately, in our culture and society, the pure rainbow spectrum of color has been more fully integrated in women's apparel than in mens'. It is depressing to walk into 90% of men's clothing stores and to see a predominance of grey, black, muddy, olive–green–brown colors on clothing racks. This is another statement about how we express and define ourselves as a culture and society. These muddy colors dull the aura and actually act as a 'depressant' on the emotional and mental body, not to mention the physical. In the last few years, however, there has been a definite influx of new and brighter colors in men's fashions. It is very uplifting to see the change taking place, as more men are starting to dress in the purer colors of the rainbow spectrum.

**Light and color is neither masculine nor feminine.** All the colors of the rainbow spectrum (including all the pearlescent and irridescent colors) are pure energy vibrations of light. **In order to expand the beneficial therapeutic value of color and light, we need to RELEASE and DISSOLVE any concept or idea that certain colors are to be worn only by women and others only by men.** A New Era of Light and Color Consciousness that will increasingly expand the vital life support of each individual as well as that of our culture is emerging, as outdated, limiting, gender-role playing models are collapsing in our culture and society. This will set many people free from the unconscious entrapment of their fears, judgments and limiting perceptions. This will mark a new revolution of irridescent and pearlescent rainbow colors in clothing that will be available and worn by both sexes. We will make the shift from the denser, darker colors to the more glowing, transluscent, irridescent rainbow colors of Light. This will no doubt tremendously enhance and expand the therapeutic capacity of color and light for millions of people.

Have you ever asked yourself: "WHY DO I LIKE THIS COLOR SO MUCH?" DOES IT MAKE YOU **FEEL** GOOD? DOES IT **UPLIFT** YOUR ENERGY? IS IT **SOOTHING?** DO YOU FEEL GREATER **HARMONY** WHEN YOU WEAR THIS COLOR? DO YOU FEEL MORE **ATTRACTIVE** WEARING A CERTAIN COLOR? If there is a piece of clothing whose color really 'turns you on' and makes you feel good, then you will probably purchase it, and your answers to all of the above questions with be an affirmative **YES!** I encourage men to wear softer, pastel colors such as corals, pinks, lavenders, light creamy yellows, soft turquoise-sea green, as well as the brighter electric cobalt-royal blue, violet, ruby-violet, emerald green, turquoise, and golden-yellow colors. The lighter pastel hues will soften and expand his capacity for receptivity, love, and gentleness, while the brighter, more electric colors will bring out the vibrant light essence of his personal power and vitality.

**FOR BOTH MEN AND WOMEN:**
FOR DEPTH, GROUNDING, TRANSMUTATION, AND EX-PANDING YOUR INTUITIVE POWERS, I HIGHLY RECOMMEND WEARING A DEEP **INDIGO-VIOLET**. This color frequency is a much higher color vibration than black or grey. It will also help you to 'transmute' old concepts and limited traditional roles that are no longer healing and uplifting to the human spirit. FOR PROTECTION, AND PERSONAL EMPOWERMENT, ESPECIALLY WHEN DEALING WITH THE PUBLIC, I RECOMMEND A RICH, DEEP **COBALT-ROYAL BLUE.**

*Put a little color into your life! As you add some more colors, put some more light into the color. As you put a little more love into your heart, add some of these colors to it!*

IT WILL MAKE YOUR LIFE MORE EXCITING AND BEAUTIFUL. IGNITE THE SPARKS OF LIFE WITHIN YOUR HEART AND MIND BY SURROUNDING YOURSELF WITH ONLY THE PUREST, MOST UPLIFTING COLORS OF THE RAINBOW SPECTRUM. WITNESS YOUR MOODS LIFTING, YOUR ATTITUDES SHIFTING, AND YOUR EMOTIONS **CELEBRATING!**

## THE LIGHT ESSENCE OF COLOR THERAPY
**Color is never separate from Light itself.** Without light there would be no life, and we would not be able to appreciate or enjoy anything visually. Light is the sustaining life force of the universe, and that same energy sustains the life of our physical body. There are many different frequencies and forms of light energy. The physical sun and stars make up a variety of gases that are one aspect of light. Within each living creature is another more subtle frequency of that same universal light essence. This is the light that is generated within the electrons as they spin around the atom. Even within the atom there is a spark of light that gives it life and movement. Science and technology have proven that the human eye can only distinguish a small, infinitesimal part of the color-light spectrum that exists in our universe. What this means is that most human beings are only able to see and distinguish the six basic colors of the rainbow and their combinations, tones and hues, which can be in the thousands. Beyond this limited visual sense perception exist millions and billions of exciting irridescent and shimmering frequencies of color and light that are not yet visible to the human eye.

During any healing process, the color that is most frequently used or visualized is white and green. Not only is white light the color of purity, but it also contains all the colors of the rainbow spectrum. Just think what a dull world it would be if we could not perceive even the few precious colors that we are able to see on this earth plane? Take away color, and you take away the vital life force, and what you have left is a very dull, drab world. Most people who are not color conscious or aware of its potent, therapeutic values simply follow the current fashion, rather than create their own personal, creative value system that expresses the colors that are healing and uplifting for them.

During the autumn season, all the commercial clothes racks are full of completely drab and dull colors. Wintertime gets even worse. Does that mean that we too have to become drab and dull, and loose our 'luster' for life because of the fashion industry trends? There are times in the winter season (where I live Northern California and Oregon area), when there are days and weeks of grey, depressing weather. It is a time when the dark grey, low pressure clouds seem to hang in the atmosphere for days. During these depressing weather conditions, one may not see the sun for days or even weeks. When this happens, I especially like to wear clothes whose colors are vital and uplifting to my spirit. It definitely helps balance and uplift my mood and emotions from a state of greyness and depression, to one of light, joy, and vitality.

I also enjoy wearing different gemstones that help activate the frequency of the particular light ray I am working with. Natural gemstones such as AMETHYST, CLEAR QUARTZ, CITRINE, TOURMALINE, TANZANITE, ROSE QUARTZ, KUNZITE, and AQUAMARINE, are just some that will enhance and amplify specific light frequencies that are healing and uplifting. For example, when I am working with very dense or negative energies, I choose a rich, deep, brilliant amethyst pendant, ring, or crystal. It has great powers to dissolve, transmute and clear accumulations of very dense energy. This gemstone also amplifies all activities serving the Light. If I need to expand my powers of communication with someone or myself, it helps to work with amazonite. When emotional balancing and nurturing is needed, or when I wish to expand abundance in my life, I choose a beautiful, clear, golden citrine pendant. The same conscious awareness that is used in choosing a special gemstone or crystal for self-healing, balancing, or beautification, can also be applied to the clothing you wear and what colors you have selected for your home or work environments.

Let's consider the clothes we wear. This has the most immediate and direct effect on our emotions, body, aura and self-image. THE MOST HEALING COLORS THAT LITERALLY EXPAND AND BEAUTIFY YOUR AURA ARE THE PUREST COLORS OF THE RAINBOW SPECTRUM. These same colors can also be worn as soft, pastel tones. Soft pastels radiate a gentle, open, receptive and loving energy into your aura, while brighter, more electric colors energize your aura and add confidence to your creative expression. These brighter colors are especially helpful to wear if you are more introverted, shy, have low self-esteem, or have a difficult time expressing yourself freely. Since there are so many shades, tones, and hues of color and combinations to choose from, it is really helpful to have a basic color reference guide (See Color Plate 3 and 4 ) to conveniently access the healing properties of each color in order to select which ones will be most beneficial for your mental, emotional and physical state at any given time. ONE PRIMARY AND BASIC REFERENCE

GUIDE I LIKE TO UTILIZE IS THE PURE CRYSTAL–WHITE LIGHT SPECTRUM. **The color radiance you see emanating from a diamond or a crystal is the most pure essence of light and color as ONE element.** When you look through a prism or a clear crystal, you see the purest of colors in the form of pure, rainbow light energy. (See Color Plate 4) When you look at a beautiful mother of pearl shell, you see the same pure rainbow colors except they are milkier, softer, and more pearlescent. You see the same colors, but as a brighter, more intense, irridescent version in an abalone seashell. Become aware of your moods, by starting to "tune into" what kind of colors and energy you need in your personal space to enhance how you feel. When you need a softening of energy, choose soft mother of pearl or pastel colors like turquise, pink, lavender, violet, blue, sea green, and pale cream colors that contain a pure shade of white. When you need energizing or need more vitality, choose the more brilliant, abalone colors.

The colors I do *not* recommend using are muddy, low energy colors that have either black or murky browns and greys mixed into them. There is nothing wrong in wearing black if you feel very introverted, self-contained, or if you feel you need more protection from the outside world. If you are in a more introverted mood, another color that is even more effective to wear for protection is cobalt royal blue or indigo. HOWEVER, WHEN BLACK DYE IS MIXED INTO ANY COLOR, IT DIFFUSES THE PURE ESSENCE AND LIGHT OF THAT COLOR. **This results in a color that generates less life force essence and lacks the vitality of the pure rainbow light spectrum.** Most colors 'on the market' today, contain some proportion of these darker dyes as they appear in clothing stores, hospitals, furniture stores, offices, airports, restaurants, classrooms, schools, and other institutions. Just think of how many shades of blue you have seen. I am particularly fond of pure royal cobalt-blue. Do you know how difficult it is to find a piece of clothing of this pure color, especially in a natural fabric such as cotton, rayon or silk? And who wants to wear polyester on their skin, when the millions of skin cells cannot breathe through this artificial material made of oil and plastic? Most blue shades on the market are all dyed with black or grey, and as a result, they lack the pure lustre and brilliance of the blue rainbow spectrum which is such a vital color of protection, energy and will. **If you are low in energy, and need more vitality, choose to wear the brighter abalone rainbow colors. Colors that are stimulating and energizing are magenta, pink, electric-blue, ruby and gold.**

Try these various color combinations and you will begin to notice how different you feel. Be playful, have fun and be imaginative. You can choose varying degrees of hue intensity, such as wearing brighter, more brilliant colors on the lower part of your body (skirts, pants,) while wearing softer more pastel colors on your torso (blouses, tops, shirts, etc.) Or, you can reverse the two, depending on what you sense your body needs. Don't let the weather or outer circumstances around you stop your own creative choices. Be yourself. Be daring. Be playful, and have fun! Stay away from dull, muddy, murky colors, as these lower the vibration in your auric field. SURROUND YOURSELF WITH ONLY THE PUREST ESSENCE OF THE THREE PRIMARY RAINBOW COLOR SPECTRUMS (See Color Plate 4).

Make some changes in your environment, such as creating new curtains, sheets, bedding, bathroom towels, etc., and of course, your own wardrobe. As you learn more about the healing properties of color, light and gemstones, you will natually become more creative and playful with your choices.


## REMEMBER:


**ALL COLOR IS A SPECIFIC FREQUENCY OF LIGHT ENERGY.** On the following page, I have created a chart of the THREE PRIMARY RAINBOW COLOR SPECTRUMS that are the most healing and have the highest vibration of harmony and light frequencies on this planet.

# THE THREE PRIMARY
# RAINBOW COLOR SPECTRUMS

## HIGHEST PURITY, HIGHEST LIGHT ESSENCE
## and MOST HEALING

*Please consult Color Plate 4 for the color photographs illustrating these three color spectrums.*

1. THE COLORS OF THE PURE RAINBOW SPECTRUM OF LIGHT AS SEEN THROUGH A DIAMOND, PRISM, OR A NATURAL QUARTZ CRYSTAL.

2. THE IRRIDESCENT RAINBOW COLOR SPECTRUM FOUND IN AN ABALONE SEASHELL OR HIGH QUALITY FIRE-OPAL.

3. THE SOFT, PEARLESCENT RAINBOW COLORS FOUND IN A MOTHER OF PEARL SEASHELL.

The above three categories of color are the purest, most healing, and uplifting color-light frequencies on planet earth. In application, feel free to interchange between these three, depending on your personal needs, your mood, or what aspect of your personality you wish to enhance.

# 27

# TWENTY–SIX STEPS
# TO IMPROVE GLOBAL AWARENESS

See Chapter 31, page 246

# PART V

# TECHNOLOGY, SPIRITUALITY
# AND
# GLOBAL AWARENESS

HITO-

TSU

UNI

WORDS FOR **ONE** LANGUAGE

UNE

EIN

UNO

EIJN

# 28

# COMPUTER TECHNOLOGY, COMMUNICATION, AND THE HEALING ARTS

## INTRODUCTION

Being a professional recording artist these days requires the use of some pretty sophisticated technology. I remember starting out over ten years ago, with just very simple and basic recording equipment. Today I record my music into a computer. This enables me to have greater control over the refinement and perfection of the music. In many ways this has opened up a new dimension in my creativity, since I am working so much with computerized electronic equipment and upgraded, computer software. I am able to attain greater precision out of the recording process. I can change any specific note, making it shorter or longer, alter the harmonic pitch, etc. This is very important, especially when orchestrating other layers of instrumentation and sound effects, as the alignment and timing of the notes must be completely in synchronization with the notes on the other tracks. The computer program also gives me tremendous editing capability. It's much like using a color palette that can always be changed and adjusted with new tones and colors added or taken away. Almost every single piece of electronic equipment in my music studio is a 'computer-chip' system. All the various synthesizers and sound effect units are interconnected through a system called MIDI Interface. They all converge into this main system via computer together with monitor, keyboards, recorder and mixing board. At first I do all my recording, fine-tuning and editing on the computer, and then I transfer the data on to either a digital or analog recording system.

On one level, this freedom of refinement and precision is wonderful, but on another level, some of the spontaneity may be lost in the editing process. By being aware of these technical limitations of the electronic medium during the editing process, I have learned how to retain the warmth, spontaneity, and human sensitivity of FEELING as I record a piece of music. At times this has been extremely challenging, to the point where I just want to smash the computer. It is at times, a love-hate relationship, and this is another aspect I am learning to master and refine. The way I think, feel and compose is sometimes so different from how the software programs function. I constantly have to learn to readjust my focus and thinking process in order to adapt to the particular design of the software without compromising my artistic integrity. What really takes place is that I am interfacing with the mind and consciousness of the person who created the software program. Most of these programs are designed to function in a more linear, logical, mathematical and sequential manner, which is generally left-brain oriented. This is challenging to an artist who is primarily right-brain oriented (intuition, spontaneity, creativity). However it is a welcome balance and becomes a valuable process in integrating the two hemispheres and activities of the brain. THE BEAUTY THAT I FIND IN THIS PHENOMENA IS THE POTENTIAL MARRIAGE BETWEEN ART AND SCIENCE.

The process of interfacing with the consciousness of the software engineer creates a certain degree of flexibility and creative expression that allows the artist to explore greater musical possibilities. At the same time, this technical matrix creates certain boundaries and limits that I must learn to understand in order to utilize the maximum range of possibilities that this creative medium offers to me as an artist. When purchasing a piece of electronic or computer software, I carefully choose one that will give me the least boundaries for my creative expansion, a program that is specifically developed and designed with the needs of an artist in mind, rather than those of a computer scientist. I became aware of another very interesting phenomena in dealing with computer systems. It is their tremendous sensitivity to human input, and the state of consciousness of the individual operating the equipment. There were times when I didn't feel that great and started working on my computer. Sure enough all kinds of jams and problems started to generate on the screen!

My friend *David MacKay*, who is a computer specialist, repairs Cat-scans in hospitals. He shared that through his experience and observations, the negativity and greed of the doctors and technicians would many times literally impair the normal function of the Cat-scans. **Learning how to effectively and harmoniously interface with computer technology is an important step in creating harmony and cooperation with any electronic medium of communication.** It may help us a lot to just sit down, meditate, and clear our energy before even turning on a computer. A computer may function much like a quartz crystal, that **receives, transmits, and amplifies** the information, input and signals sent by the person. **Perhaps once we understand the inner mechanics of our own nervous system and how it functions in relation to the different stimuli it receives, we may be able to interface our own organic electro-magnetic circuitry with that of refined computer systems in a much more effective and harmonious way.** The ideal technological synthesis would be for a brilliant scientist, engineer, or physicist to have a clear understanding and respect for life, creation, and human development. Having refined these values and qualilties, his or her intention and purpose in form of a newly developed technology, would then be clearly directed toward expanding life support systems that would benefit all life on the planet.

It is fascinating to note that there are precise, mathematical relationships that correspond to the musical scale and the theory of harmony. *Pythagoras*, a great teacher who lived during the classical Greek period, taught that all harmony is based on a pure mathematical set of relationships that can also be found in nature, i.e. in a sound wave, in light, in color, and in music. **When an artist or musician is aligned with the harmonic frequency of the universe, he will transmit a resonance that will have the same corresponding vibratory frequency that already exists as a mathematical relationship of universal harmony.** Certain tones when played in combination with one another, create a new series of overtones which set up another level of unique mathematical relationships, and as a result we hear a new, harmonic resonance.

I am particularly interested in the electronic medium of sound and communication. Electronic sound 'transmits' electrical energy much like a beam of light. It is pure energy in motion. It really doesn't matter whether a sound is created from an acoustic instrument such as a piano, violin, or a flute. Both these and electronic instruments are created by human hands, with a Divine Mind and Heart guiding these manifestations into form. **All sound is vibrational energy expressing itself through motion** creating a resonance in the space in which it vibrates. What I enjoy so much about working with electronic music is the Uranian aspect of transformation and acceleration. Certain electronic frequencies of sound are most effective in transmuting and dissolving denser forms of energy that 'get stuck' in our mental, emotional and physical bodies.

**The electronic frequency of sound, when consciously directed, has an immediate effect on denser forms of energy, by dissolving the crystallization pattern that has caused the blockage in that area.** As the blocked energy is dissolved and released, a new, more accelerated vibration of light and sound energy creates a more open and expanded resonance field that contributes to our healing and to the vital re-balancing of all our energy centers. THIS IS WHERE TECHNOLOGY AND SPIRITUALITY MEET. There is a continuous readjustment of two minds. The scientist or engineer who is creating these sophisticated computer software programs, has to adjust and tune into the 'intuitive' process of an artist's right brain function. In turn, the artist-musician is learning to fine tune and perfect his own perception pattern and organizational skills by starting to learn more about the logical, sequential patterns and relationships that will support and refine his creative vision. It is a two-way, reciprocal relationship. Both minds must meet each other half way in order to receive the highest benefit of the technical medium. This mutual process allows for a major, and

transforming shift in the relationship between the technical communications media and the healing arts which
will reveal many powerful new discoveries that will
benefit all of humanity in the very near future. **The
flexibility and combination of consciously–directed
intention and the desire to create instruments for communicating love, beauty, healing, education, and
human transformation that is life-supportive, will usher
in a new age of technological and spiritual development for humanity.**

Many brilliant discoveries by genius scientists and
physicists become misguided and greatly abused by governments, corporations, and military establishments who
manipulate these discoveries for their own destructive
purposes.   HOW WE USE AND DIRECT THE TECHNOLOGY
THAT WE HAVE AVAILABLE TO US TODAY IS THE KEY
THAT DETERMINES THE FUTURE LIFE OR DESTRUCTION
OF OUR PLANET.

The potential benefit that technology has to offer
humanity is tremendous. We have only touched the tip
of the iceberg. In the following pages I have interviewed
four key people who utilize or work with technology
extensively in their careers. I have consulted with them
regarding their interaction and experience with technology, and asked all four the same questions in order to get
their personal 'feedback' on specific issues that regard
the nature and direction of technology in its relationship
to spirituality and human development. Here is a list of
the following four people that I interviewed and their
professional field of specialization:

*NORMAN B. MILLER* is co-founder of Rainbow Research Inc. which is dedicated to research and education

in the fields of music, light, color and positive imagery. He is founder of the new Holistic Spiritual Science of Electronic Alchemy. Currently he is working as writer and producer of the IMAX movie *FUTURE QUEST*. He also developed the concept and is co-director of the *GLOBAL ACTION PLAN*, (a California non-profit corporation) which is a comprehensive organizational map and world-wide movement for turning the tide of ecological deterioration on our planet through economic conversion and sustainable development. Participants include the UNITED NATIONS, NASA, IMAX FILM CORPORATION, Friends of the United Nations, and various other corporations, small businesses, and individuals.

*DAVID MACKAY* began his career as an electrical engineer specializing in computer architecture and bio-medical applications. After many years of studying eastern medicine he began to understand how spirit directs matter through the operation of the subtle bodies. He is currently an advocate for the creation and development of self-sufficient spiritual communities and technologies which aid in humanity's spiritual evolution.

*KEN JENKINS* is the award winning creator of numerous videos, most notably *ILLUMINATION* , a visual musical video, and *INNER WORKOUT* by Shirley MacLaine, which features a half hour of kinetic mandala images for chakra meditation. Ken has also contributed to and assisted with more than a dozen other videos and films. For seven years he was an editor and technical director with Hewlett-Packard Television. In 1990 he was presented the Crystal Award at the Second International New Age Music Conference for his contributions to the emerging field of visual music. He is currently in pre-production on a New Age science fiction movie.

*IASOS* is an electronic music creator and is one of the original founders of "New Age Music", releasing his first album in 1973. His specialty is celestial music. He has been doing multi-media concerts, incorporating special color effects and visionary paintings by many fine artists since 1970. In all his work, Iasos' motto is: **"Advanced Technology for Sacred Purposes"**. He has won numerous awards, both for his music and his video work, including the Crystal Award for 'Artistic Achievement' at the International New Age Music Conference in Hollywood. The underlying purposes for all of Iasos' work is to give people an audio and visual experience that will assist them in contacting higher realms of Light and their own inner Divinity.

# 29

# THE INTERVIEW:
## TECHNOLOGY, SPIRITUALITY, AND HUMAN DEVELOPMENT

All four people that were interviewed were asked the same questions, so you will see four different answers to each of the eight questions:

1. DO YOU FEEL THAT OUR PRESENT TECHNOLOGICAL ADVANCES ARE REALLY CONTRIBUTING TO THE WELFARE AND LIFE SUPPORT OF THE INDIVIDUAL?

*Norman B. Miller:*

I would have to say that generally, technological advances go to support the interests of corporations, governments and businesses that represent the status-quo. These businesses, whether they are in health care, electronics, energy, transportation, etc, are mainly developed around these organizing principles: **To maximize profits, maintain control of markets, generate power and to perpetuate this control through social and political influence.** The individual, on the other hand, is seen as a 'consumer' to be listened to through demographics, to get the product right, to make the most sales. In the end, it is those of wealth and power who have the resources to implement these technologies, who benefit the most in our society. If there is any doubt of this reality, all one has to do is go to the downtown areas of our larger cities and take a look at the large numbers of 'throw-away people' this society has created. It's ironic that the very industrial revolution which was supposed to free humanity of physical drudgery has been so successful that now large segments of our population remain alienated from the economic life force of our society, and the polarization between the 'haves and have nots' is becoming greater and greater.

*David MacKay:*

All technology is a reflection of the consciousness that creates it. If the motivation of those who are developing technology is to truly be of service to humanity, then that technology will be beneficial for those who it is intended for within that particular time and application. If the motivation for technology is greed or the desire for power, then only a select few will temporarily benefit, while many others will have to deal with the present and future negative impact of the technology. **Because of mankind's current, limited awareness, the true and long term effects of our technology cannot be foreseen until our awareness expands. So even something that is created with the most noble intentions can have negative effects on the environment because of our ignorance.**

Each generation creates a technology which it perceives to be a panacea for all its social ills. The succeeding generation inherits it and builds upon the positive aspects and seeks to mitigate the consequences of the negative aspects. As awareness continues to expand, technology becomes a tool which aids in the expansion of that awareness. The massive global communications system we have created is a very powerful tool whereby all of humanity can be connected and the highest aspirations of the species can manifest. Unfortunately, because of the fear, greed, and desire for control, this system is often used to divide humanity, or to keep us unaware of the divine potential existing within all of us. The majority of the resources of most nations are currently spent in the development and acquisition of military systems. This only reinforces the underlying fears and insecurities in the mass consciousness and produces a highly unstable world situation. When humanity realizes that the true basis of its nature is spiritual and not physical, then the majority of our fears will dissolve and we can truly begin to manifest our highest aspirations.

*Ken Jenkins:*
(The following answer applies to questions 1, 2, and 3.)

Technology is neither positive or negative. It is neutral, like electricity or fire. It can be used to help or harm, at the discretion and free will of the individual(s) using it. As a result of those free will choices, our present technological advances are **both** contributing to and benefiting individuals and people in general **and** hurting and harming people, because some individuals choose to abuse the increased powers that technology provides. The point is that technology itself is not to blame. The responsibility lies, as always, with the individuals who create this technology and how they use it.

## 2. ARE PEOPLE IN GENERAL OR 'HUMANITY AT LARGE' BENEFITING FROM THIS TECHNOLOGY?

*Norman B. Miller:*

The question of whether humanity at large is benefiting from technology is a very complex one and could easily be the topic of an entire book. The answer depends on where you stand in the economic spectrum. A.Z.T. for AIDS patients has proven to relieve symptoms and improve the length and quality of life. Yet many people cannot afford this drug and so they continue to suffer. If you live in a third-world country, it's largely unavailable to the average person. The same is true of most state-of-the-art, medical technology. Computers were supposed to make our lives easier, but have they really? What they have done is added a greater level of complexity to our society. In talking with an unemployed office worker, she complained that she used to find plenty of jobs based on her typing skills. Now she has to know Word Perfect, Lotus 1,2,3, Harvard Graphic, etc. (computer software programs), have a high degree of computer skills, etc., and she still makes no more money comparatively than she did in the 1960's before the computer age 'kicked in'.

How this added complexity makes us feel 'inside our gut' is a question we rarely ask. Is high tech Los Angeles a better place to live today than it was in the 1930's? According to my parents (who have lived in the Los Angeles area for over sixty years), the answer is an emphatic NO! And then there is the question of what technology is doing to the life force of our planet. And yet, I see the seeds of hope, greater consciousness, and the ideals of sustainability springing up all around me. The major question is whether these seeds will be allowed to grow to fruition, or will they be trampled down by humanity's rush for profit and greed?

*David MacKay:*

In order to fully answer this question one would have to analyze thousands of separate technological developments and their effects upon society. One can say however, that any technology which aids in expanding our awareness and knowledge of ourselves as spiritual beings provides the greatest benefit to individuals and society. The telephone, television, and modern communication systems are all technologies which have simultaneously expanded our knowledge of the world and reduced the cultural and geographic boundaries between all of us.

Communication is the most powerful consciousness expansion tool we have, and any technology which increases the quantity and quality of communications will benefit humanity. Information processing and dissemination technologies can be highly beneficial or destructive depending on the intent of those controlling the main network of information systems. Simply by selecting and controlling the information 'fed' to the public, the people can be led to enlightenment or worldwide genocide. This was shown very clearly in pre-war Germany and has the potential to occur in many current nations. Each individual is now making a choice as to how they interact with and utilize the tools that are available to them. If within their hearts they truly desire to be of service in creating a better world for all of us, then the power of that desire will attract the tools which will help them to make that choice a reality.

3.  DO YOU FEEL THERE IS ANY ABUSE IN HOW THIS TECH-
    NOLOGY IS BEING CHANNELED, OR WHERE IT IS BEING
    DIRECTED?

*Norman B. Miller:*
Technology is like a hammer. It can be used to build
a house or it can be used as a lethal weapon. To which end
we use technology is determined by economics, politics,
and ultimately the consciousness of individuals. **Even
though we have come to the end of the Cold War era, we
still qualify our essential life's energies through the
social matrix of the military-industrial complex.** This
must change, and FAST for the sake of our country and
for the sake of all life on our planet. We are living in a time
where abuse abounds in almost every aspect of our lives,
from the Rodney King beating to insurance "gouging", to
an economically, corporate-controlled stock market,
public healthcare in shambles, democracy besieged by
special interest groups and trillion dollar deficits. These
are disastrous trends that cannot go unabated. One last
example, as I write, the number **one** and number **two**
most popular movies at the Box Office this week are
*SLEEPWALKERS* by Stephen King which depicts incest,
disembowelment, and cruelty to animals, and *BASIC
INSTINCT*, a film about a woman who slashes men to death
with an ice-pick at the moment of orgasm. What greater
havoc and abuse has technology caused than what we
willingly impose upon our own collective psyches? **Outer
reality is only a projection of our collective inner reality, and it is from this point of awareness that all
negative and positive arises.**

*David MacKay:*
There is currently tremendous abuse of how the political and corporate structures of each nation direct

technological development. The forces of greed and fear are the prime motivators for how much of the resources of the world are abused. The political systems of many nations disregard the needs of the citizens and have directed their resources to develop technologies which will ultimately be used for the destruction of life and nature. Ultimately every dollar spent on weapons technology incurs a karmic debt which leads to the spiritual and material impoverishment of society. The money spent on a single bomber could feed, house, and educate thousands of children who now live in poverty without hope for the future. The callous disregard for the most basic needs of the meekest members of society, while the tremendous gluttony of the military and corporate structures continues to be sated, can only lead to a two tiered society, a super wealthy minority which controls resources and an impoverished majority which can only be controlled through economic and physical violence. Ultimately all social institutions will collapse because of the tremendous misuse of power.

Technology which poisons the air, food, and water for the greed of the multi-national corporations creates an overburdened and collapsing healthcare system which can no longer handle a nation of ill and imbalanced citizens. Media programming which appeals to the lowest common denominator causes a spiraling decay of the morality and consciousness of the viewer, until all are reduced below the level of animals. Television has the potential to enlighten all of humanity, but is instead used as a tool for social control and manipulation, only furthering the desires of the greedy and the power hungry. Highly unsanitary and dangerous energy production systems continue to be built by corporations, while the development of clean, safe and inexpensive energy systems are hindered and crushed at every opportunity. The "think tanks" (corporate jargon) which develop policy options for the nations are funded by the multi-national corporations which are concerned only with their profits and nothing for the welfare of the citizens, environment, or the spirit of humanity. The vast majority of technological development is now being directed by corporations simply to increase their profits. This has a devastating effect on the environment and can only result in the material collapse of society. Technological development must be directed from an attitude of service to humanity in harmony with nature and respecting the spiritual source of all creation. This will once again put humanity on the path of expanded awareness, love, and harmony with all of God's creation.

4.  DO YOU FEEL THAT THERE ARE MAJOR TECHNOLOGI-
    CAL BREAKTHROUGHS AND DISCOVERIES THAT ARE
    NOT MADE PUBLIC? AND WHY?

*Norman B. Miller:*
    The best and most complete way I can answer this question is to suggest to the readers that they rent or purchase the videotape, THE SECRET OF NIKOLA TESLA. It is available at many metaphysical bookstores that also carry video rentals. The story as outlined in this movie is played out every day in our business world, only the faces and technologies are different.

*David MacKay:*
    There are many major discoveries which are never made public simply because they would disrupt the profits and control of those who direct world economic activity. So-called 'new' technologies will be introduced

into society in a manner which will minimize world economic disruption and maximize profits. Simple, clean energy systems exist which can provide all our energy needs. Implementing these systems today would cause widespread economic displacement which would ripple through the entire world economic system. We have the technology to switch from a highly polluting, and dangerous oil/nuclear economy, to a clean and safe solar/hydrogen economy. The money now spent on bloated military budgets could easily cover conversion costs. However, any potential threat to existing corporate profits will not be tolerated even if it means poisoning all life on earth with foul air, water, and food. There is much evidence to suggest that anti-gravity and non-polluting fuel-less energy sources exist. Individual researchers in these areas are denied patents because they are too much of a threat to the existing scientific paradigms and corporate profits. Eventually these breakthroughs will be too numerous to be controlled, and the individuals and corporations that risk disrupting the status quo will eventually become the new industry leaders.

*Ken Jenkins:*

Yes, I think there are cases of technological breakthroughs and discoveries that are not being made public, either for economic, social reasons, or both. I am not sure that it is quite as widespread as some suspect, since most such breakthroughs would benefit the holder economically, and therefore would be released. In my opinion, two examples are the mythical 100 MPG carburetor I believe is just that, a myth. The laws of thermodynamics prove that such a device is simply impossible. On the other hand, there is the possibility that breakthroughs in solar energy have been bought up by the oil industries and withheld to protect their profits. Considering how often large industries exploit people for profits, it is safe to assume that some technological breakthroughs are withheld.


**5. HOW WOULD YOU IMPLEMENT A TECHNOLOGY 'FOR THE PEOPLE'?**

*Norman B. Miller:*
  Now this is the type of question I like, and one we should all be asking. Through my work with the GLOBAL ACTION PLAN, UNITED NATIONS ENVIRONMENTAL PRO-GRAM, NASA, etc., I have given a great amount of thought to this question.  Again, the answer could fill an entire book (or video/audiotape). **The answer has to do with shifting our social, political, and economic priorities out of the military industrial complex and into new systems of energy which are life supportive, following the principles of nature, and truly filling the needs of individuals and the life force of the planet.** In essence, humanity needs to be reborn, and in my opinion, the impetus for this rebirth will come through the rallying cry of "HELP SAVE OUR PLANET". The U.N. is now preparing for an Earth Summit on the environment  in Rio de Janeiro, Brazil. They are compiling environmental information and data from around the world. The picture that is being painted for the near future is more apocalyptic than even the most informed person had imagined. This picture includes an increasing amount of ozone erosion, drastic increases in skin cancer, disruption of growing seasons with a potential for mass starvation, the possibility of dying plankton on a large scale, (base of the food chain in oceans), increased desertification, possibility of increased infra-red exposure that blinds insects thus creating large 'brown-out' areas due to lack of pollination,

etc. The GLOBAL ACTION PLAN has been created to deal with these serious problems through a comprehensive, highly integrated systems approach which utilizes mass communications, education, new technologies, and input from smaller businesses, enlightened corporations (Yes!, there are some, and awareness is growing day by day), concerned individuals, and government officials. (For a copy of the GLOBAL ACTION PLAN, see 'Note' at end of this chapter.)

*David MacKay:*

Gandhi was one of the first world leaders to talk about technology "for the people". He reintroduced the spinning wheel to the villages of India to make the people much more self-sufficient and reduce the need to import cloth from England. As long as technology remains centralized and under the control of profit motivated individuals, the potential for abuse continues. A technology "for the people" must be decentralized so that 'each individual' has control over the technology. Massive urban centralization makes people highly dependent on sophisticated food, water, energy, and resource delivery systems. When these systems operate in a responsible and efficient manner, all citizens profit from the maximum utilization of shared resources. When the operation of these systems is driven by short term profit, then urban survival itself becomes an issue as each of these systems becomes overburdened and collapses.

**Appropriate technology emphasizes more self-reliance and a simplicity in living that seeks to increase the quality of life through creating more fulfilling, spiritual relationships with those around us and the natural world.** By teaching the values of love, nurturing, respect, harmony, and peace, people gain far greater joy by exchanging the love in their hearts than they could from possessing any material object. Each person becomes responsible for his own health, well being, and success in life as opposed to being dependent on society for all of his or her needs. Technology and material life would continue to evolve, but in a direction in which material aspects would serve and complement the spiritual aspect of the human self and not dominate it. **Implementing technology "for the people" first requires that people be educated about the options available to them. Showing them that a much higher quality of life is possible within a much simpler lifestyle gives them a choice of how to direct their energy.** People could provide most of the food and energy requirements for their own community from local sources. Independently owned, self-reliant franchises could provide the local area residents with information on how to develop everything they need to create a self-sufficient community. This would make it possible to create a highly sustainable, decentralized society which is not vulnerable to excessive manipulation by the corrupt few.

*Ken Jenkins:*

The key to implementing a technology "for the people" is creating easy access, especially user-friendliness. We live in a time of rapid change and advancing telecommunications. With home computers, interactive cable, faxes, CD-I's, and so on, becoming so common, the challenge is to create ways more people can access and more readily use these technologies. With the advent of the personal computer allowing individuals the power and convenience once available only to large corporations, a big step in that direction was taken. Another major step will be the proliferation of interactive cable to homes via fiber optics. Once it is enough widespread, there will be such things as electronic referendums and polls, and eventually voting done in the home. This will be a major step in making representative governments truly "of the people". But to make it really work, it must be so user-friendly that the vast majority of people can use it. It must be as basic as a cable television remote control. Fortunately, technology is getting to the point where computer systems are increasingly 'transparent' to the user, so the goals are more achievable. The other key to access this wonderful potential is, of course, cost. People must be able to afford the services and devices so that they can become more widespread.

## 6. IS THERE A RELATIONSHIP BETWEEN SCIENCE-TECHNOLOGY AND SPIRITUALITY?

*Norman B. Miller:*

There can be a direct relationship between science, technology and spirituality. Most obviously, technology can free people from drudgerous and repetitive work, so they may have extra time to pursue the higher aspirations of life. There is, however, another dimension to technology that is rarely explored because we have not yet freed ourselves from the problems expounded upon in earlier questions of this interview. The example closest to my heart is the new 'holistic spiritual science' of Electronic Alchemy which I have developed over the past twenty-two years of research. This science utilizes music, light, color, positive imagery, sacred geometry, and knowledge from wisdom traditions throughout time and delivers them through state of the art technologies to assist in new breakthroughs in human consciousness and enlightenment. The perfect delivery system for this science has been developed. . . It's called VIRTUAL REALITY and I look forward to working in this new format in the future.

Another example is the new educational delivery system of multi-media where text, pictures, graphics, sound and real time video are all integrated as one into the learning process. Through the use of this new technology we will be able to see how one thing is related to everything else. It tends to break consciousness out of the 'linear mould', and into a new spherical paradigm. I contend that this way of looking at reality could be interpreted as a spiritual experience. I'm sure that others are working in similar fields of endeavor which will also prove important to the spiritualization of humanity.

*David MacKay:*
    Technology is an exact reflection of the spiritual condition of humanity. The most revolutionary aspects of technology today are in the computer and electronics industries, as well as the biotechnology field. During the industrial revolution, mankind created many devices to take the physical drudgery out of life. We invented machines to do the manual labor in life, thus freeing ourselves from being laborers. Now we are developing tremendous information processing capabilities very similar to the tasks handled by the left hemisphere of our brain. First we created machines to take over the physical labor and now we are making machines to take over the mental labor. Two hundred years ago the most common occupations were farmers and laborers. Now, in the highly industrialized nations, clerical, information processing, and service positions are becoming the most

common. Computers linked with automation will take over the majority of these positions over the next hundred years. Intelligent machines will replace the physical and mental drudgery of life. Mankind will be free to explore the unused potential of the right hemisphere. This part of the brain directs all activity associated with creativity and the exploration of inner space. An entirely new society with highly expanded awareness and universal values will appear, with individuals manifesting abilities not yet accepted in our current world views. The biotechnology revolution represents man's desire to create new life forms which he deems beneficial to his needs. With tremendous arrogance and ignorance this field moves forward developing new species purely for short term profit. This will have disastrous long term effects upon the environment simply because it is impossible to predict the biosphere's adaptive response to such alien organisms. When we look at the overall cumulative effect of all new negative and positive technologies, we see that tremendous alterations in the biosphere will occur as it tries to adapt to the application of these technologies on a mass, global level. This will lead to the disruption of world weather patterns, food production, species survival, human immune response, and every other area of life which was highly stable and predictable at one time. **The greatest need of human development right now is for us to recognize and respect the spiritual interconnectedness of all life and to understand the effect that humanity's consciousness has in the creation of life.** As the misuse of technology threatens the very survival of our species over the next twenty years, the consciousness of a slumbering humanity must either awaken or perish.

*Ken Jenkins:*

To answer this question, I must start by giving my definition of spirituality. Spirituality is our relationship with God/Goddess/All-That-Is. By that definition, since science and technology are part of All-That-Is, there is clearly a very direct relationship with spirituality. Our entire universe and everything in it is a part of God/Goddess/All-That-Is. Science, at its root, is a search for knowledge and understanding of ourselves and the universe, and is, at its heart, a part of our search for God-All-That-Is and for ourselves.

7.  IS THERE REALLY SUCH A THING AS A 'NEW' TECHNOLOGICAL DISCOVERY OR IS IT SOMETHING THAT WAS ALREADY DEVELOPED ON OUR PLANET MANY THOUSANDS OF YEARS AGO, POSSIBLY IN ATLANTIS OR IN OTHER CIVILIZATIONS?

*Norman B. Miller:*

I prefer not to speculate on the past. I would rather project my vision into the future.

*David MacKay:*

We are spiritual beings evolving through a material universe. **All science and technology manifest the desire for control over physical existence.** Ultimately, all technology further separates humanity from God in that people place their faith in material illusion instead of spiritual reality. However, as man is a physically incarnate being, material evolution can be hindered or advanced through technological developments. Technology and material life become a tool for focusing and directing humanity's energy. The harshness of physical existence becomes a challenge through which man learns to manipulate the environment by developing and focusing the will. Humanity learns to master the mind, will, and desires in order to achieve a more secure existence. **It is not the technology itself which is of prime importance in our existence, but the mastery of self which is gained through developing the technologies.**

Science and technology can greatly assist humanity on the spiritual path. By expanding our awareness of ourselves and the universe we inhabit, humanity gains a perspective on the order of the cosmos and our relationship to it. Systems which increase communications between individuals and nations help to foster greater understanding and compassion between diverse elements of human society. Mass media can educate society in the ways of peace, love, and understanding for all living beings. Science and technology can also destroy all of humanity and greatly retard human evolution. Negative television programming can put us to sleep or actually degrade the morality and consciousness of the entire human race. The by-products of technology, pollution, species extinction, destruction of health and natural resources, definitely hinders mankind's spiritual development. But these problems also call forth an inner strength from many individuals in society who commit themselves to the solution of such catastrophic, global problems. These individuals who take on these tasks begin to manifest the highest potential within themselves, thus rapidly advancing their own spiritual evolution. Therefore even the most negative impacts of technology can bring about a spiritual birth for many members of society. Ultimately, material science and technology will be obsolete, for we will all learn to work with the energies of spirit directly, and our souls will have mastered all the challenges of physical existence.

*Ken Jenkins:*
I think the answer is both: some discoveries are genuinely and totally new, and some 'new' discoveries are really 'rediscoveries' of technologies developed in Atlantis and elsewhere. These were carried forth and further developed in other civilizations such as ancient Egypt, the Mayans, etc. In my opinion, I don't believe that there has been such advanced development of micro-electronics in history, but other areas, such as crystal energies, were much more highly developed in Atlantis.


8.   WHAT IS THE DIRECTION OF TECHNOLOGY IN RELATION TO HUMAN DEVELOPMENT?


*Norman B. Miller:*
**The consciousness of most people in the industrialized world runs thirty to fifty years behind what is possible technically and scientifically.** The great challenge for humanity now is to close this gap so we may truly utilize our human ingenuity to solve pressing problems, while at the same time living a balanced and healthy life. Then there are the rare few, the visionaries, who have learned to consciously 'ride the wave' of syncronicity and merge with what will be possible in the future with the higher aspirations of humanity. And then, here's the RUB. . . those who are ruthlessly devoted to maintain that which IS without question or concern for further human development. At this critical time in history, it's of great importance that each of us realize where we fit into this spectrum and challenge ourselves to do better.

## David MacKay:

Certainly the technology we are currently developing is 'new' to those who are discovering it. Many researchers and authors suggest that all the technology we currently have and even more advanced technologies existed in previous civilizations including Atlantis. There is archaeological evidence which supports that ancient cultures have had electricity, nuclear weapons, and even space travel. There are radioactive, fused-glass ruins in India suggesting the possibility that a nuclear war may have happened many thousands of years ago. Perhaps all we are discovering today is simply ancient memories being recalled from the collective unconscious. If this is the case, then we must proceed with the greatest possible caution because the last civilization to possess this knowledge obliterated itself so completely that humanity has lost all trace of their existence. Let us educate each other in the knowledge of spirit and the responsible use of technology so that we may avoid a similar fate.

## Ken Jenkins:

Technology is a mirror for human development. As our consciousness expands in awareness, so does our technology along with everything else. So I see the direction as being parallel, one a reflection of the other.

## Iasos:

(As he felt more comfortable in expressing himself through an essay form, the following interview with **Iasos** answers all eight questions within a single exposé, inter-relating the eight different questions into one answer).

To discuss the relationship of technology and spirituality, I feel a need to see this within a broader relationship
of the political, economic, and the technological system,
and then the consciousness and spirituality of that culture. From a sociological point of view, the political
structure is based on the economic structure, and the
economic structure is in turn based on the current technology. And, the state of the art technology is the result
of the consensus reality or 'group consciousness' of that
culture. This 'group consciousness' is the result of the
average level of spiritual development within the people
of that culture. Let's diagram this relationship:

SPIRITUALITY → CONSCIOUSNESS →
TECHNOLOGY → ECONOMICS → POLITICS

When viewed from this perspective, it becomes clear
that the spirituality and the consciousness of the people
is the CAUSE, and that the technology/economics/poli-
tics is the result. Now, to momentarily "pop-out" of this
local point of view and see it from the point of view of the
space beings (extraterrestrials) that have been visiting
and closely observing our planet. From *their* point of
view, our planetary culture is seriously imbalanced
because **our technological evolution is significantly
more advanced than our spiritual evolution. This means
that we have the tools and means to create powerful
*effects* without the spiritual wisdom to properly *guide*
these tools.** This is analagous to letting a four-year old
child drive a jet air-liner, and the results are equally
dangerous. It is insightful to know that the space beings
representing the ASHTAR COMMAND, which is working
very closely with the spiritual hierarchy for our planet,
has, since the days of Eisenhower, contacted the political

leaders of all the major world powers, and have attempted to lovingly offer their introduction and assistance by helping the development of our planetary culture. And without exception, ALL of the political leaders chose NOT to inform their people of these higher developed civilizations. The leaders were obviously afraid that they would lose their power with their people, if the people would become aware of other forces more knowledgeable than their own leaders.

Equally interesting is the fact that consistently, these space beings have pointed out repeatedly to all these governmental heads that our spiritual development is dangerously *behind* our technological development, and they have lovingly offered to assist us in spiritually "catching up" to our current technological level. And sadly, in all cases, the political leaders had NO interest whatsoever in gaining any spiritual wisdom from these highly evolved beings, but instead, only wanted to greedily gain any and all technological "tips" and information that they could. In other words, our leaders are not "hearing" these warnings that our technology is dangerously more advanced than our spirituality. The warning that we have developed very powerful tools without also developing the spiritual wisdom to properly and effectively implement these tools to benefit our planet is clear.

If these space beings have such an advanced technology and want to help us, why don't they just share their technologies with us, so we can feed the poor and house the homeless? In their higher wisdom, they have good reason to withhold their technologies: If you look back at our diagram, you will see that if you *suddenly* introduce a new technology, this cataclysmically changes the economic structure, which in turn shatters the political system based on this economic structure. These extraterrestrial beings do not wish to shatter our economic and political systems. Like the 'Prime Directive' in Star-Trek, they do not wish to cause planetary chaos by meddling unwisely in other people's affairs. Also, any technology is neither good nor bad. It just IS. Any technology can be used or abused. You can use electricity to destroy life or to create comfort by warming a home. As long as our planetary propensity is to use the "state of the art hi-tech weaponry", like "smart bombs", the space beings will wisely withhold their technology until we reach a greater spiritual maturity as a planetary community.

Now, zooming back to the American culture, we can see that there are many inventions that are potentially of *profound* benefit to the people, but these inventions are being 'held back' as politically "forbidden". Referring back to our diagram, we see that politics is based on economics, which is based on the technology. So, if the current technology creates an economic system, where certain powerful forces are making tremendous financial profit, then these powerful forces will use their economic power to influence the political structure, so that the political structure "outlaws" any new technologies that would threaten the current, economic power system with its tremendous financial profits. In other words, the economic systems which are currently the most influential (that is, making the most money) will use their power to cause the political system to *force* the technological "status quo" to remain as is. Consequently, new technologies of tremendous, potential benefit are squelched and held back, since their introduction  would cause tremendous financial loss to those corporations and financial institutions currently making phenomenal profits from the current technologies. For example, in America, pain reduction clinics are big business and clinics to dissolve addictions are big business. Intelligent individuals who have studied electronic devices that facilitate certain beneficial frequencies into the body through the skin ("TENS" devices), have studied their uses throughout the world and noted their extreme efficiency in reducing pain and in quickly removing addictions of all kinds. These intelligent individuals have designed small devices that are the size of 'Walkman' cassette players and that could sell for less than $100 each. They innocently and hopefully went to numerous health clinics to introduce them to these newly developed devices, thinking that such health tools would further the intention of these clinics. To their surprise, they were laughed at and mocked,"*What? We're making $15,000 -$18,000 for each individual that stays in our clinic for two weeks, and you want us to give all this profit up just so we can sell them a $100 device? Are you crazy? Also, these individuals keep coming back to our clinics, and if your device really does work, then after the $100 sale, we would never see them again. Get out of here! We don't want to know about your device at all.*"

Perhaps the technology with the greatest "taboo factor" is "free energy". Since, if this were implemented, it would mean disastrous financial losses for the big energy companies, like P.G.&E., etc. Nikola Tesla, with his technological genius, was economically naive. He thought it would be a great thing to make free energy available world-wide. As soon as his benefactor J.P. Morgan found out what Tesla was really trying to do, to make "free energy" available globally, he immediately 'pulled the plug' on the funding for all of Tesla's projects, and without funding, Tesla's dreams for free energy never materialized.

These examples underline the fact that, **as long as our current spiritual level of evolution is such that the** *profit motive* **of personal ego is stronger than the** *service motive* **of the transpersonal self, then the current political system will always resist new technologies that are potentially beneficial,** since this would mean a restructuring of the economic system and therefore a tremendous loss of profits for those financially benefiting from the current economic system. This means that significantly new technologies that are of tremendous benefit can infiltrate into the culture ONLY IF the economic structures that are already making huge profits can incorporate these new technologies into their own financial businesses. That is, if these big corporations can implement and financially benefit from the new technologies, they will be allowed to be released into the culture. But if the big companies CANNOT financially benefit from these new technologies, these threatening technologies are suppressed, and made "taboo" and illegal.

Fortunately, consciousness and spirituality are the CAUSE, and technology the effect. And there IS is a current planetary up-shift in consciousness that is occurring steadily, globally, and irresistibly. **As this CON-SCIOUSNESS trend continues, more and more people will be thinking of how to apply technology in ways that benefit others.** **As this planetary up-shift progresses, there will be a major shift in the collective orientation of humanity from the PROFIT MOTIVE FOR PERSONAL GAIN to the SERVICE MOTIVE FOR THE BENE-**

FIT OF THE WHOLE. As this shift in consciousness continues, this will become the predominant mind-set rather than the exception. And at that point, the political structures globally will no longer resist beneficial, new technologies. At that point, the whole of society will wholeheartedly welcome any and all such beneficial technologies, and we will be quick to embrace and implement these into our culture.

TECHNOLOGY is a reflection of CONSCIOUSNESS, just as all behavior is a reflection of consciousness. As this planetary up-shift continues to accelerate in momentum, there will be less concern for personal gain and more interest in benefiting the whole. There will be less concern in profiting at the expense of others (like profiting from cutting down the Amazon rain forests) and more concern with an ecological awareness of the inter-dependence of all life on earth. This will mark a major spiritual transformation in humanity. And as this spiritual awareness continues to blossom globally, more people will be inwardly motivated to create tools that serve, heal, uplift, and benefit others. And just as a mirror unfailingly reflects light, this loving, caring, *conscious intent* will manifest in the caring technologies of our New Earth.

## TECHNOLOGY'S FUTURE QUEST

Once we learn how to utilize the great gift of life that we have been given by healing the cause and effect of all self-abuse, we will begin to re-pattern our evolutionary blueprint by accelerating the pattern of perfection in which we were originally created. When we collectively as a human race stop abusing ourselves, nature and the life around us, I do believe that at that point, we will have available to us a technology that will reflect the pristine purity of our intentions to love and respect all life forms as well as our own. Life serves you when you learn to serve life.

When we reduce all the unnecessary stress and negative stimuli of the media within our personal lives, and heal our nervous system and addictions, we will be able to tune into finer frequencies of light and sound that will assist us in making that quantum leap into teleportation and tele-communication systems not only on this planet but with other planets, galaxies, and solar systems. Once this Grace flows freely again within each individual, there will no longer be a need for doctors, hospitals, lawyers, police, insurance companies, or military systems. Naturally, the whole economic system will be irrelevant and useless, since each being will have mastered the laws of cause and effect by learning how to govern his or her own lifestream harmoniously and by respecting all of life. This will allow each being to instantly manifest whatever he or she needs for life support through the process of precipitation without depending on any external source or power. The brilliant discoveries of scientists like Nikola Tesla could revolutionize the entire planet within a decade, starting today! There are hundreds of other discoveries already made waiting 'to come out of the closet' for the benefit of humanity. **The big lesson is that we must first "clean up our own act and backyard" sufficiently before we can have the added benefit of such great power, a power that we must learn not to abuse or misuse as we have done before on this planet.**

We are rapidly approaching the quantum leap in our planetary evolution as more and more people awaken to their own inner potential. There is no way that any government or corporation in the world can manipulate or hold back any longer the growing light within so many people. When enough people in this world create this inner light resonance frequency, the economic and political systems will have no choice but to adjust by serving the light and life of each individual's highest potential as well as that of humanity. At this level, we may begin to implement a new technology whose purpose and function truly supports the expansion of light, health, love, peace, harmony, prosperity, intelligence, and the liberation of humanity.

Note:
If you are interested in ordering a copy of the *GLOBAL ACTION PLAN* (See page 223), please send $25 (check or money order, $30 outside the U.S.) payable to: Norman Miller, P.O. Box 6987, Laguna Niguel, CA. 92677

# 30

# GLOBAL AWARENESS

## NO MAN IS AN ISLAND UNTO HIMSELF

You've probably heard the expression, "No man is an island unto himself." As human beings, we are all interconnected not only to one another, but to all life forms on the planet, such as the vegetable, mineral, and animal kingdoms. We are an interdependent species who rely on one another for our survival. Without the trees and vegetable kingdom, we would not have the necessary oxygen to breathe. Without water we would die of dehydration, and without the sun, there would be no life on this planet at all. Sadly enough, one of the things that is most lacking in not only our present modern culture, but in many other cultures around the world, is a basic awareness of what is happening on the rest of the planet. Most of the time each country focuses on their own national problems and rarely expresses a care by tapping into what's happening in other countries around them or globally. We are still living in an isolated, divided, ethnocentric, nationalistic world of individual cultures and religions. We have become so disconnected from one another and nature, that we have lost our sensitivity and the AWARENESS of life's essence. Driven by blind ambition and greed, the old patriarchal system has completely lost sight of how perpetual abuse is affecting the entire planet and its citizens. Instead of working harmoniously with nature, man's will has abusively 'projected' his own brutal willpower in order to manipulate nature for self-aggrandisement, raping our planet of her natural resources, polluting her environment, creating major holes in the ozone layer, a myriad array of diseases through chemical germ warfare and toxic drugs, allowing mass-starvation, the splitting of the atom and even withholding important cures that have been discovered years ago. How do these various forms of planetary abuse and negligence affect each one of us? How does it affect life itself? What does it say about humanity's 'collective' respect for life? For ourselves?

Many of us are so preoccupied with our own personal problems and life's daily challenges, that we lose sight of what is really happening around us and on the rest of the planet. Being informed about global conditions and their consequent effects on life means learning to be conscious of the whole and how it is affects every one of its living creatures. With all of our resources, communication systems and technology, isn't it amazing that we are allowing 40,000 children to die of starvation each day! Just think that with every other breath, another child's life is extinguished for lack of food and/or medical care. How does this phenomena affect life within the cells of our own body? What kind of effect does this energy have on our own sub-conscious mind, and 'collectively' for the mind of humanity? Just stop a moment, and feel the reality of this situation, then you will begin to feel and appreciate the life force within you and what a precious gift life really is.

In order to raise the quality of life on our planet, each person must come into their own personal awareness and sensitivity for the preciousness of all life, treating it with the greatest love and respect. This is a start, and as your own life-essence becomes purified and honored by a personal self-care program, you can then begin to reach out to less priviledged beings by doing something that will truly help another human to have a chance in life. There are various international children's agencies where you can sponsor a child for only twelve dollars a month. That's only forty cents a day! What a difference this small amount can make for someone who is on the edge of life.

The assistance and reaching out to others doesn't always have to manifest in the form of money. It can be volunteer services in order to help the environment, lending a loving hand in hospices, health care programs, or learning to recycle plastic and glass. **By simply becoming aware that by eating red meat, we are directly contributing to the extinction of the precious rainforests. Since more fields have to be grown to feed more cows that are later slaughtered for meat, it is depriving our planet of the vital oxygen and good air that we so desperately need for our health.** Eating red meat also contributes greatly to major heart diseases. **The depletion of the natural balance of oxygen in nature is also contributing to the holes in the ozone layer.** To take this a step further: Are you aware of how many toxic, poisonous chemicals and drugs are injected into animals to make them fatter before they are slaughtered? The real 'shocker' is that this is not only being done to animals, but indirectly to human beings as well if they are not careful or conscious about what they are putting into their bodies. Instead of supporting life, the 'name of the game' is to poison people with toxic chemical preservatives to get

more people into hospitals, keep the insurance companies going, and interest rates up by increasing the amount
of debt. Doesn't this say something about the quality of
life in our present, modern culture?

### FUTURE GLOBAL EARTH CHANGES
I'm sure you have heard of some earth changes, such as
earthquakes, tidal waves, etc., that are predicted for the
very near future. There is a lot of speculation about these
upcoming, major earth changes that may be quite intense
and devastating in the next few years. Since there has
been such pronounced abuse of the earth, her peoples,
nature, and her resources, there are times in our planet's
history when the earth physically releases a tremendous
amount of pressure from within her inner core in the form
of earthquakes, tidal waves, etc. This is indeed how the
continent of Atlantis sunk into the ocean. As the conti-
nental shifts continue, and the polar ice caps melt, the
earth and all her elements are dramatically and critically
affected.

For clarification, I am certainly not ENERGIZING any of
the predictions or the belief that we should panic. However, I DO believe that it is very important to be aware of
the POTENTIAL HAZARDS and POSSIBILITY of such major
earth changes taking place in the next few years, especially around 1997. The most intense physical earth
changes will occur on the West Coast of the United States,
since this is the location of the major fault lines. This may
not be a safe area in which to live in the next few years.
About a week ago, I had a very powerful experience. As
I was writing a chapter on the Eight Light Rays, I had just
typed into the computer the following words, "... AND AS
THE OLD WORLD CRUMBLES. . .", when immediately my
desk started to shake, the computer shook, and I looked

244 AWAKENING YOUR INNER LIGHT

over to the window and my hanging plants were swinging and the floor and walls swaying. At first, I thought I was just getting dizzy from working too long on the computer. Then I realized that this was a real earth tremor. We felt the shock of the 6.9 Richter Scale earthquake that devastated Ferndale (near Eureka, California). Then at around 4:30 a.m. the following early morning, another tremor hit the town of Scotia. Needless to say, when I read the phrase that I had typed into the computer and, then *directly and immediately* experienced the tremors as the phrase was complete, it certainly was a dramatic and major sign of warning and awakening that made me poignantly aware of what the near future may hold.

There are many ways that the earth can clear herself of all the negativity and abuse that has been projected unto her collectively by all of humanity, whether consciously or unconsiously. We have reached such a *critical mass* of human discord that, at times, the earth can no longer withstand the tremendous amount of accumulated energy and pressure created by this human discord and abuse. However, I also believe that at the present time, there are millions of lightworkers living on our planet who have the ability to 'collectively' generate a powerful focus of Light, Peace, and Harmony that can **neutralize** and *transmute* the potential destruction of life that threatens our planet at this crucial time of her transformation. It may be wise however, to be PREPARED AND READY, if major earth changes do take place, especially since we have had recurring major trickles of tremors in California in the last few years. There are many books written on this subject, available in both bookstores and libraries, if you wish to learn more about the fault lines and the geological activity of these potential 'danger zones'. I highly recommend that you include the earth and all of humanity in your healing visualizations, affirmations, prayers, and in your meditations. To help the earth transmute all the negativity and discord, it is helpful to visualize the following healing meditation for the earth:

### EARTH HEALING
### MEDITATION AND VISUALIZATION

Visualize the earth surrounded in a radiant, deep violet light. Then visualize a pink light glowing around the violet in order to magnetize increased love energy into the planet. After you have surrounded the earth in the pink light of divine love, you may then put a deep cobalt blue light of protection around the pink to neutralize any discordant energies around the earth's atmosphere. As a final touch, you may wish to surround the cobalt blue with a glorious and brilliant, radiant essence of white and gold light to seal the earth in the light rays you have invoked for her healing and transformation.

**It is also wise to remember, that before we can heal the earth, we must first learn to heal ourselves. As we increase the focus of our own personal human development and continue to implement greater self-help care programs for healing ourselves and others, it will automatically help heal and raise the energy vibration of our environment, as well as to set an example for global transformation.** When we have healed, mastered, and transformed all levels of self-abuse, realizing our True Self and I AM GOD PRESENCE to be ONE WITH ALL BEINGS, we will automatically approach the earth with greater love, reverence, respect, and gratitude for the life sustaining energy and beauty she provides us, by giving her the loving care and respect she deserves.

# 31

## TWENTY-SIX STEPS
## TO IMPROVE GLOBAL AWARENESS

What can we do to raise the quality of our own life? Here are some following, practical suggestions that will increase the life support system within your own body and on the earth:

1.  AVOID RED MEAT.
    Eliminate it completely from your diet.

2.  AVOID REFINED WHITE OR BROWN SUGARS. There are healthy alternatives such as fructose, date sugar, honey, and maple syrup which can all be purchased at a health food store, and some of these items are also available in regular supermarkets.

3.  ELIMINATE WHITE, BLEACHED FLOUR from your diet completely.

4.  AVOID EXCESSIVE COFFEE, ALCOHOL, AND DAIRY PRODUCTS.

5.  If you live in a large, air-polluted city, go out once a week to a  place that has clean air.  Practice deep breathing as you inhale the fresh air into your lungs

and body. Visit spas and steam-saunas to clear and open your lungs and the pores of your skin.

6 . DON'T WATCH TOO MUCH TELEVISION! IT IS DETRIMENTAL TO YOUR EMOTIONAL, MENTAL, AND PHYSICAL HEALTH. Choose inspiring programs that are life-supporting, not life-threatening and abusive.

7. AVOID EATING CANNED FOOD. Do not eat foods that have chemicals and preservatives added to them. You can obtain a book on food additives in any major bookstore. This book will inform you which preservatives or food additives have been sufficiently tested, and which are safe for human consumption. When I read Ruth Winter's *"A CONSUMER'S DICTIONARY OF FOOD ADDITIVES'*, I was shocked to learn that most chemical preservatives were not sufficiently tested but were released anyway, regardless of whether or not they caused cancer or abnormal growth in laboratory animals.

8. SHOP MORE AT HEALTH FOOD STORES, and eat as much ORGANIC produce as possible. ORGANIC FOODS ARE FRUITS AND VEGETABLES THAT HAVE BEEN GROWN NATURALLY WITHOUT THE USE OF PESTICIDES AND CHEMICALS. They always taste much sweeter and flavor-full, and of course are much healthier.

9. STAY AWAY FROM TOO MANY FRIED FOODS. Baking is healthier, or a light stir-fry using a cholesterol-free oil like Canola or Sunflower Oil in a stainless steel wok.

10. DO NOT COMBINE FRUIT AND VEGETABLES DURING THE SAME MEAL. Wait 30-40 minutes either before or after a meal. The same with water or other liquids. DO NOT

drink with your meals, since it dilutes your digestive enzymes, causing indigestion and gas. Drink only pure water. Do not drink city tap water. Get a water filtration system. Water is as important to your body as breathing good, fresh air. Drink at least 7-8 glasses of pure, filtered water a day. This helps flush out all the toxins that we absorb from pollution, chemicals and additives, etc. Make it a habit to drink one large full glass of water as soon as you get up in the morning before having your coffee or tea.

11. Eat some live, raw food daily, like a small salad or fresh fruit, nuts, raisins, sunflower seeds, etc.

12. AVOID MICROWAVE OVENS. The radiation destroys the healthy nutrients and vitamins that your body needs.

13. DON'T EAT WHEN YOU ARE EMOTIONALLY UPSET.

14. PRACTICE 'SAFE' SEX.

15. GET TO KNOW YOUR PARTNER FIRST, BEFORE YOU JUMP INTO BED WITH THEM.

16. Learn to channel your sexual energy by allowing it to flow through your whole body, feeding all your cells, without the need for a physical orgasm. Conserve your sexual energy as much as you can, without suppressing it. Learn to channel and re-circulate your passion by doing the tantric chakra-meditation exercise. (See page 23)

17. Go for outdoor walks at least 4-5 times a week. Practice some form of exercise that you really like, such as swimming, hiking, bicycle riding, etc.

18. IF YOU NEED PROFESSIONAL HEALTH CARE, I highly recommend CHINESE MEDICINE. Acupuncture, Chinese herbs, and other natural alternative health care such as ayurveda, homeopathy, and wholistic health centers.

19. DO NOT SUPPORT OR GO TO SEE VIOLENT MOVIES whose themes glamorize terror, violence, fear, suspense and murder. This is detrimental to your mental, emotional and physical well being.

20. Practice some form of MEDITATION or SELF-AWARE-NESS program to expand your inner development. Create some time just for nurturing yourself by doing something that helps you relax and unwind. For instance, this may be listening to soft, healing and uplifting music, or reading an inspiring piece of literature or poetry.

21. BE AWARE OF YOUR SURROUNDING ENVIRONMENT. Plant some trees around your house. Create  a nice vegetable or flower garden.  Take more time out to commune with nature, just by physically being in a natural environment with more trees, mountains, rolling hills, forests, rivers, lakes, oceans, etc. Express your gratitude for the life and support that nature gives us.

22. DON'T USE FLOURO-CARBON SPRAY CANS that are destroying our planet's ozone layer.

23. SEEK OUT ALTERNATIVE NATURAL SOURCES OF ENERGY SUCH AS SOLAR, WIND-POWER, ETC.

24. BECOME AWARE OF HOW YOUR ACTIONS AND VERBAL EXPRESSIONS ARE AFFECTING THE REST OF THE PLANET.

25. Share your resources with others by giving something meaningful back to life. Donate a percentage of your profits to a charitable organization.

26. Seek out others of 'like mind' with whom you can openly share and communicate your ideas. Allow yourself to really express what's inside your heart and mind by learning to be more open in your communication with loved ones. You may find that there are surprisingly many more beings like yourself as you learn to reach out and create a strong supportive network and links of communication locally as well as globally. There are many international organizations such as GREEN PEACE, the SIERRA CLUB and UNICEF, that you can join to offer your own special contribution to raise the quality of life and consciousness on our planet earth.

# PART VI

# EPILOGUE

MUSIC IS BOTH THE PERSONAL AND
TRANSPERSONAL LANGUAGE OF UNIVERSAL
LIGHT, LOVE AND DIVINE INTELLIGENCE
THAT TRANSMITS NEW FREQUENCIES OF LIGHT
AND SOUND VIBRATIONS THAT HAVE THE POWER
TO HEAL, UPLIFT, AND TRANSFORM
HUMAN CONSCIOUSNESS.

AT THIS LEVEL,
THE SOUNDS ARE NOT JUST MERE MUSIC,
BUT A VIBRATIONAL FREQUENCY OF LIGHT AND
INTELLIGENCE THAT IS RESTRUCTURING THE
ATOMIC AND CELLULAR PATTERN OF
OUR HUMAN EVOLUTION.

# 32

# THE NATURE AND ORIGIN
# OF THE MUSIC I COMPOSE

Music is both personal and universal. It can express such a variety of feelings, moods, visions, inspiration, and it can also be very healing. Everyone has their own range of what they like or dislike according to the development of their emotional, mental and etheric body. Unfortunately, the unlimited, expansive range of cosmic universal music has not yet permeated the mainstream market or humanity at large. However, major breakthroughs are taking place globally as more and more gifted artists and musicians are beginning to be recognized and acknowledged for their great musical genius. There is an increasing wave of light and intensity on our planet. As the struggles and conflicts within each human being are *acted out* on the screen of daily life, it is amplified and reflected back to us through the mass-consciousness of humanity. This results in an increasing polarization of energy on our planet during this present time of our human development. As the polarization between light (love, wisdom, healing) and darkness (ignorance, abuse, disease) intensifies, each being must make their own personal choice whether they wish to serve the Light or drown in the illusion of fear, negativity and abuse of power. One can see this tremendous polarization in the modern rock and pop music that is on our planet now. One can also see this major abuse in the media especially television programming and the motion picture industry. The quality of consciousness that is amplified through music or film can and does influence millions of people. It can either have a positive, healing, uplifting effect, or a very negative, harmful, self-destructive one, depending on the content, intention and consciousness of the person creating the music or film. It is also the public, the audience who buy and support these movies and music, that collectively create either a positive healing effect on our planet, or contribute to the conflict, abuse, and self-destruction that is so prevalent in our media today. It is the choice of each individual to decide what level and quality of consciousness they wish to embrace and support.

**Sound and light are the two universal forms of energy that permeate all creation, not only in our galaxy but in other dimensions as well. Sound and light carry a vibration of INTENTION, WILL, PROJECTION, and PURPOSE.** Sound is the auric emanation of Light. The two are never separate. Light and sound can create, heal, or it can destroy. Once again, it all depends on the INTENTION AND DIRECTED WILL of the person sending out their own particular vibration into form. The intention (often unconscious) could be to express rage, anger, conflict, hatred, terror and fear, or (when consciously directed) express harmony, joy, love, beauty, peace, expansion, transformation, and spiritual upliftment.

Music can express a tremendously wide range of feelings, emotions, and thoughts. Unfortunately, a lot of modern rock and heavy metal music today is not 'consciously' created, and very little or no regard is paid to the purpose, intention, and the effect that this music will have on the listener. Many musicians and composers are afraid to express the spiritual side in their music, in fear that it will not be accepted by the public. There is a lot of pressure of fitting into a *marketable groove*, which becomes the main thrust and purpose of most of these musicians. So, within this limited range of predetermined concepts of what the public will like and what *sells*, becomes the limiting foundation for the creation of the music.

As people learn to reclaim their own personal power and identity, they will redirect their energy in a more conscious way by developing greater discernment that will allow them to make wiser and healthier choices. This will result in a major breakthrough and transformation of the entire music industry as well as the motion picture industry. As more and more people heal their own personal emotional-mental conflicts and begin to heal the illusion of duality within their own consciousness, they will no longer resonate to music and films that perpetuate a discordant vibration of conflict, fear, and self-abuse. **As the mental and emotional bodies of humanity become more refined and healed, they will start to align themselves with energy and sound vibrations that will assist them in 'tuning into' more expanded and universal states of consciousness.**

## HOW I GOT STARTED COMPOSING MUSIC
In 1979, as I was completing a painting entitled, *MUSIC OF THE SPHERES*, (Color Plate 7) I received an important inner message. Since I have been developing my painting and airbrush technique for over ten years, I was able to create unique transparent tones of color and light frequencies that interplayed with one another. During the

creation of this painting, I started to hear inner sounds that corresponded to the tones and frequencies of the colors and light in the painting. At that point I realized that if can do this with color, light and form, I should be able to bring this same harmonic frequency through the medium of sound and music. During this time, I also received the transmission of my new name AEOLIAH. The painting I was doing had a harp in it and the strings where made out of light rays. There are also a lot of spheres (planets) in the painting and pure rainbow colors. My vision was to create a harmonic interplay between the spheres and the light rays of the harp (which is also partially spherical), as this interplay created varying degrees and tones of rainbow light and color. As the painting was nearing completion, I realized that the subject matter of my painting was very much connected to an Aeolian harp, (a musical instrument created during classic Greek Era) which was a large stringed instrument (long rectangular) that would intentionally be placed outdoors so the wind would actually play the strings. This resulted in natural tones and overtones of sound. . . a music that is literally played by Nature. This became known as the wind harp and the sounds that would emanate from this instrument was associated with the Music of the Spheres. That is how I received the transmission of my new name.

I still had no idea when or how I would start to create music until I returned from a trip to Hawaii in 1980. A few days after I arrived in California, I received an inner message that said, "You are going to bring through a musical album that will amplify such healing qualities as mercy, compassion, forgiveness, and all-embracing love. You will be assisted by the Goddess Kuan Yin (Chinese goddess of mercy and compassion) who will be by your side as you bring this album into manifestation." My instant reaction was, "This is absurd, I'm not a musician, I'm an aritst. How am I going to achieve this, where do I start?"

All the circumstances that led up to the actual experience of recording my first album, INNER SANCTUM were very magical and definitely guided from higher planes. A recording studio was provided effortlessly, electronic instruments, and even a beautiful harp manifested at the perfect time when I needed one. During the process of creating INNER SANCTUM, I learned how to 'walk' on different ground. It was very challenging, exciting, and beautiful all at once. I also gratefully received the assistance of wonderful friends who were present to support and encourage me during its creation. It was like learning how to swim, ski or sky dive. Great lessons of trust and learning to 'let go' of the ego became instrumental in shaping this music. A major lesson was learning how to become a clear vessel to allow this music to pour through me and to become One with it.

As I started releasing my concepts of 'being in control' and learning 'to go with the guided flow', I started experiencing great beauty and a magic that was guiding my every step. Needless to say, it was a very healing experience on many levels as well as emotionally challenging, since I was just going through a major separation from a marriage. The day before my scheduled final mixing session in the recording studio, I called my wife in Hawaii and, to my surprise, I was informed that our relationship was over. Naturally I was emotionally devastated and in a state of shock. There was no way my physical and emotional body could handle going into the studio the next morning to complete this album. I simply could see no way I could do this. As I booked the studio weeks in advance, and was flying back to Hawaii the day after the scheduled final mix, I was really faced with a challenging predicament. I started praying for help and once again an inner message said, "You will go into the studio tomorrow and you will complete this album". During that night I experienced great conflict and pain and could hardly sleep. The next morning I automatically started to get ready to go to the studio. When I arrived, I was 'in the dumps', and even during the mixing session, I would burst into tears as I was completing this first album. As I was releasing so much emotional energy, the music became a powerful tool to help transmute a substantial amount of  pain in my emotional body.  The concentration and focus that is required, as well as surrendering to the guided flow of the music during the mixing session, facilitated the transmutation of a tremendous amount of my own emotional pain and trauma.  By the time I left the recording studio, I felt a major shift in my energy. My emotional body felt a lot lighter, and even though I was still experiencing some pain, the music had definitely lifted a lot of the heavy emotional  energy I brought into the studio.   **I later realized that I was enacting the transmutation of my own human pain and suffering into a more universal aspect of my  Self through the help of the music, whose qualities of compassion, mercy, forgiveness and all-embracing love became my healing balm.**  A couple of years after the release of *Inner Sanctum*, it was revealed to me that the transmutation process I experienced in the recording studio was an initiation not just for my own personal evolution, but that I would assist many others in 'transmuting' and raising their energy and vibrations through new music I would compose in the near future.

Another  major  breakthrough  in  my  musical  career
occured in 1985 when  I released  *ANGEL LOVE* (See front
book  cover  image,  and  Appendix).   At  the  time  I  was
living in Mt. Shasta, California, which is one of the major
spiritual power points on the planet. It was the first time
that I started to write out each note as I was composing,
rather than improvise like I did on my first two albums
(*INNER SANCTUM and THE LIGHT OF TAO*).  This was a very
new experience for me, since it involved more left-brain
coordination and greater self-discipline combined with
staying open to the spontaneous, intutive (right brain) aspect of the creative process.  During the creation of *ANGEL
LOVE*, my vision was to create a piece of music that would
radiate  and  transmit  the  purity  of  angelic  feelings  and
emotions. I wanted the world to have a taste of the purity,
devotion, and unconditional love of the angelic kingdom
and  their  incredible  service  to  humanity.  I  remember
staying up until four  in the morning completing the mix
of this album in the same recording studio where I mixed
my first album. (Mixing is a technical process that com-
bines  all  the  separate  tracks  that  were  previously  recorded 8, 16, 24, 36, tracks or channels of sound.)  It is
during this crucial stage of combining the right levels of
each  recorded  track  and  carefully  shaping  each  sound
that becomes a critical and challenging process demand-
ing undivided attention and care. It requires great focus
and concentration to achieve this delicate balance, refinement, and subtlety of tones that transforms the music into
a living, completed entity.  During the mix of the second
piece,  (*Celestial Sanctity*)  I  strongly  felt  the  presence  of
Mozart  in  the  recording  studio.  It  felt  like  he  was  right
behind  me  and  inside  me  as  he  was  guiding  my  fingers
and hands on the control panels and faders of the mixing
board.  I felt enfolded in an overwhelming love vibration
as this master presence guided me so lovingly and gently.

A true state of Grace resulted in this effortless mix. I was so deeply moved by the love I felt, that once more, tears became part of my mix. However this time not from pain, but from the joy and ecstacy of pure unconditional love.

When I arrived home at around four-thirty a.m. I was so completely 'wired', I could hardly sleep. So I took a hot bath and then went to bed. It was then that I received another incredible transmission. It was more than just a dream. I was on the side of a snow-covered mountain in Greece, and next to me was a beautiful white winged horse with a soft pale pink hue throughout its white body and mane. As this beautiful horse approached me, the message was clear for me to mount it. As I did, this graceful white-pink pegasus spread his wide wings and gently we ascended around the top of the mountain in a spiral three times, and then, very gently, we landed back on the side of the mountain where I first arrived. This dream stayed so vividly in my mind and memory as I woke up later that morning, that I decided to find out more about the symbolism of this visionary dream. I found a wonderful book on dream interpretations (*WATCH YOUR DREAMS* by Ann Ree Colton) and found the section that listed the dream interpretation of a white winged horse. It read the following: "INITIATION INTO THE HEALING ARTS AND THE FIFTH RAY OF HEALING, **ARCHANGEL RAPHAEL**." As I read this I became so excited and blissful to know and receive CONFIRMATION that my vision for the creation of *ANGEL LOVE* indeed had a divinely-guided cosmic purpose and was directly inspired and channelled through by Beloved Archangel RAPHAEL, the Angel of Healing and Consecration.

During the creation of this album, I was already consciously interacting with the teachings of the Ascended Masters and the Eight Cosmic Light Rays (See Self-Help Manual, page137,182). One of the primary rays that I utilize is the Fifth Ray, (see page 165 ) which is the Ray for Healing, Consecration, Precipitation, one-pointed focus, and the expansion of our inner third eye and Inner Ear. This Ray expands our capacity to tune into interdimensional telecommunication and trans-personal creative expression. It also expands our ability to bring this interdimensional frequency into physical manifestation through a creative form of expression such as music, art, writing, healing, channelling, etc. This process involves the opening and expansion of our pineal and pituitary gland. As we learn to develop these two centers, we will be able to not only expand our powers of healing, but also develop greater telepathy and telecommunication with higher more evolved life-forms including dolphins, whales, extra-terrestrials, ascended masters, etc. Another major activity of the Emerald-Indigo Ray is to assist us in developing our powers of creative manifestation by learning how to focus our energy in a one-pointed way to achieve the desired manifestation in physical form. Each musical album that I have released (ten at the present time), marks a specific period of my spiritual, emotional and mental development. Each album is an offering of love that also marks a major opening and breakthrough in my artistic, technical and spiritual expansion. One main focus in all my music has been to create consciously-directed music that has at least one to three primary universal expansions of the Eight Universal Light Rays (See Self–Help Manual, page 137 )

*The following Eight Universal Qualities of the Light Rays I utilize in the creation of my music are as follows in the order of my personal, artistic and spiritual preference:*

1.  ILLUMINATION–ENLIGHTENMENT–EXPANSION OF CONSCIOUSNESS AND INTEGRATION OF THE TRANS-PERSONAL SELF.
    (Golden Ray, See page 172 )
2.  UNIVERSAL LOVE (Pink Ray, See page 155)
    This one is of equal value and importance as #1 above.
3.  ACTIVATION OF SOUL -PURPOSE AND INTEGRATION OF ALL THE SEVEN RAYS (Mother of Pearl Ray, See page177)
4.  HEALING and CONSECRATION
    (Emerald-Indigo Ray, See page 165)
5.  PURITY (Crystal White Ray, See page 142)
6.  TRANSMUTATION and ACCELERATION
    (Violet Ray, See page 147)
7.  UNIVERSAL PEACE and MINISTRATION
    (Ruby-Gold Ray, See page 151)
8.  DIVINE WILL, POWER, PROJECTION
    (Cobalt Blue Ray, See page160)

### THE EIGHT COSMIC LIGHT RAYS
### IN THE MUSIC I COMPOSE

1.  GOLDEN RAY OF ILLUMINATION
    One of the most predominant qualities in the music I compose is Illumination. All of my music stimulates and expands the third eye and crown centers, as well as the heart. This quality of expanding light (Illumination) is very important to me, as it brings the love energy from the heart into radiant expansion in the third eye and crown center. Everything that I teach in my seminars is contained within each recording I create. **Music becomes the transpersonal language and expression of Universal Light and Divine Intelligence that transmits new frequencies of light and sound vibrations that have the power to heal, uplift, and transform human consciousness. At this level, the sounds are not just mere music, but a**

**vibrational frequency of light and intelligence that is helping to restructure the atomic and cellular pattern of our human evolution.**

2. THE PINK RAY OF UNIVERSAL LOVE

   The primary inspiration, together and **equally** as important as Illumination, is the quality of LOVE. It is of highest importance to me that the music radiates a deep and penetrating quality of Love energy that opens our hearts, allowing us to feel safe and receptive, so we can more easily receive and assimilate the universal transmission of universal consciousness through the music.

3. THE MOTHER OF PEARL RAY

   Being able to anchor and integrate the soul plane of consciousness into expanding human awareness is another very important feature of my music. Activating and sustaining the full spectrum of all of the light rays into a harmonious integration with the mental, emotional, physical and etheric bodies, truly helps facilitate the anchoring of our Light Body into this physical dimension.

4. THE EMERALD–INDIGO RAY OF HEALING

   Another purpose of the music is to assist us in our healing process. Through its interdimensional quality of expansion, it also has to be capable of penetrating into our subsconsious, dissolving and helping to release old patterns of contraction, limiting belief patterns and self-abuse. As the nervous system is soothed by the healing vibrations of the music, a new level of trust is established between the listener and the music. This opens up a greater potential for healing and receiving sanctifying grace through the resonance of the music. Contained within this healing process is the rebalancing and integration of the mental, emotional, physical and etheric bodies.

5.  THE CRYSTAL WHITE RAY OF PURITY
    Purity of purpose, intention and integrity are in-
    valuable prerequisites for any effective healing mani-
    festation to stabilize. As the music purifies the aura of
    the listener, it automatically helps dissolve any
    mundane obsessions and stimuli of the external world,
    and helps the receiver attune to the inner realms of
    consciousness more easily. The purity of the music
    both harmonizes and raises the vibratory energy of
    our emotions, feelings, and thoughts. I work a lot with
    the white ray.  As white light expands the aura, it
    helps clear the energy field of all our chakras as well.
    In all of my music, the quality of ascending, spiralling,
    light energy is very prevalent.

6.  THE VIOLET TRANSMUTING RAY
    Together with the purity of the crystal white ray, the
    transmuting quality of the violet ray is a process that
    dissolves crystallized, old karmic patterns and raises
    the vibratory frequency of our cells to a perfected state
    of balance and well-being.  In order for this process to
    take place, **the music needs to have the accelerating
    frequency of Light to 'step up' and raise the vibra-
    tory rate of our emotional, mental and physical
    bodies.** This acceleration process allows transmuta-
    tion to occur, as the denser forms of self-judgment,
    denial, resistance and other forms of self-abuse dissi-
    pate in the presence of this healing resonance. Violet
    is also the most rapidly vibrating light ray of the color
    spectrum, so it has the greatest potential and power to
    accelerate our transformation.

7.  THE RUBY–GOLD RAY OF PEACE
    The soothing and calming balm of universal peace
    balances our entire endocrine and nervous system.

When the music has this soothing, calming effect, and is at the same time expansive and stimulating to our bodies and minds, we begin to experience greater comfort and ease as we release multiple levels of stress and tension from our being. This aspect of stress reduction and soothing calming energy is another major element in my music. When a person is in this tranquil state, they are much more receptive to the healing energies of the music. As the music opens different areas and levels of our consciousness, the dynamic balance between the soothing, calm energy and the more accelerating, expanding frequencies stimulate a higher awareness of interdimensional transmissions of light. This allows the music to act as a bridge, or doorway, into higher dimensions of soul travel. The music also serves as a sacred tool to MINISTER and transmit these refined frequencies of light energy and consicousness to humanity.

8.  THE COBALT BLUE RAY OF DIVINE WILL AND POWER
    The act of empowering  and re-energizing the life force essence through the balancing and realignment of the will center is the final aspect of the vital integration of the eight rays through the musical creation. What truly empowers us through the music is our own willingness and ability to be open to receive its healing transmission. When music helps to facilitate this process, it transmits the POWER AND WILL aspect of creation as it is PROJECTED into  physical form as pure consicousness.

IMAGINE ALL THESE  EIGHT LIGHT RAYS AND THEIR BEAUTIFUL COLORS BLENDING WITHIN THE MUSIC, RE-CHARGING AND UPLIFTING YOUR AURA WITH THE HEALING LIGHT OF THE PUREST CRYSTALLINE RAINBOW  SPECTRUM OF WHITE LIGHT.

# 33

# CLOSING STATEMENT

As you hold the VISION of your complete and total healing, transformation, and self-mastery within your heart,
remember that the spark of light within you has the
power to ignite the Light of this World.

Please know that YOU TRULY DO MAKE A DIFFERENCE,
and that every step you take toward your healing and
self-acceptance creates a new musical resonance that
brings greater harmony and joy to All of Humanity, raising the quality of life on our planet.

As more of us awaken to our True Potential, we will
add to the Light of this World and it will shine brighter as
our own Inner Light expands.

Love,

*Aeoliah*

Aeoliah

# PART VII

# APPENDIX

# PRODUCT INFORMATION

## FINE ART POSTER–PRINTS
The Visionary Art of AEOLIAH:
Each 18" x 24" (unlaminated-ready for framing)
Laminated Prints: $22.00
Unlaminated Prints: $20.00
Limited Edition, hand-signed Prints: $98.00
(Refer to Color Plate 8)

## MUSICAL RECORDINGS BY AEOLIAH
All Available as Cassette or Compact Disc

*✩INNER SANCTUM ✩* Celestial Music inspired by the Chinese goddess Kuan Yin. This recording amplifies and expands self-forgiveness, love, mercy, and compassion. Angelic voices, piano, flute (**Larkin**), harp, and synthesizers open the inner sanctum of our hearts. **#1**

*✩THE LIGHT OF TAO ✩* Cascading crystalline sounds that enfold us with refreshing waterfalls of joy and celebration as the **Sounds of the East and West meet.** A rich, harmonious and unique blend of synthesizers, lyricon (**Dallas Smith**), flute, harp, zither, electric guitar (**Doni Smith-Divino**), chimes, and sitar. **#2**

*✩ANGEL LOVE ✩* A tender angelic symphony that soothes and massages our being with a healing balm and comfort of pure joy and serenity. Angelic choir, piano, and synthesizers. Inspired by Archangel Raphael. **#3**

*☆ANGEL LOVE FOR CHILDREN ☆* A musical offering for expectant mothers, babies and children. This soothing musical lullaby is comforting and relaxing, as it harmonizes our bodies and emotions. Great for adults too! Angelic choir, chimes, bells, and synthesizers.**#4**

*☆MAJESTY ☆* Music for spiritual expansion, meditation, self-transformation and healing. Accelerates direct contact with our I AM God Presence. This music is highly devotional and expresses a deep reverence for all life. Choral orchestra, human choir, violin, piano, and synthesizers. **#5**

*☆CRYSTAL ILLUMINATION ☆* A sensational, interdimensional musical journey to balance and realign our chakras. As we progress from the base of the spine and ascend into the heart, third eye, and crown, the music builds in power and intensity. Richly orchestrated, highly consciousness-expanding music. **#6**

*☆LOVE IN THE WIND ☆* A romantic album with classical overtones of tender, delicate, and passionate love themes. A real heart-opener! Much like the classic nocturnes, with a new age twist. Piano, strings, flute, and harp. **#7**

*☆THE OTHER SIDE OF THE RAINBOW ☆* A musical anthology of six of Aeoliah's recordings plus a new featured piece with electric guitar. The musical pieces were carefully selected to create a special variety of some of Aeoliah's finest music. **#8**

*THE MAGIC PRESENCE* ☆   A wonderful new release by the multi-talented guitar-player and composer **DIVINO** and produced by **Aeoliah**. Features some of the finest electric, acoustic guitar and synthesizers played by **Divino,** interwoven with lush, vibrant textures of uplifting, harmonizing, and healing musical selections that radiate high love energy and superb artistic and technical performance. One selection, *The Open Door* , and some of the electronic space effects are composed by Aeoliah.   **#9**

*THE JOURNEY HOME: On Wings of Light*☆   A symphonic, interdimensional journey that takes us through the Stargates and Beyond. Music for personal empowerment, transformation, and expansion. Features some energizing pieces that are ecstatic and uplifting. Extra-terrestrial communication that helps access the higher dimensions. Some of this music was written for a motion picture soundtrack. The first 18-minute piece was created to heal the illusion of duality within our consciousness.   **#10**

*LIGHT AT MT. FUJI: A Live Transmission*☆   Recorded live on the slopes of Mt. Fuji, in Japan. This is the perfect music for deep meditation and for inner attunement. Transforming, healing and uplifting music of the spheres, with transparent ambience of overtones. (Recorded June, 1992)   **#11**

## THE SELF–HELP TAPES
### Guided Meditations and Visualizations with Music

These recordings are designed and created as a tool for your personal self-empowerment, transformation and healing. The text is created and spoken by **Aeoliah** and features his healing music in the background. The cassettes are highly transforming and effective, as they rebalance and reintegrate the eight energy centers of the body.

✩*LIVING IN YOUR HEART*✩ *Side One* features a guided meditation to release self-judgment, and to heal our emotional body. It activates and rebalances our heart center. *Side Two* contains transforming affirmations that assist in the healing and manifestation of our true potential and self-mastery: healing sexuality, creating loving relationships, enhancing self-worth, maintaining radiant health and prosperity in our lives. **#12**

✩*ANCHORING YOUR LIGHT BODY*✩
**Through the 8 Cosmic Light Rays: (Part 1 & 2)** This recording was created to anchor the eight universal Light Rays into the corresponding eight energy centers in the body, known as chakras. As each Light Ray is being activated and anchored into each of the corresponding eight chakras, you will experiece a powerful initiation into each of the Eight Light Rays. This eight-step program is designed for the full activation and anchoring of your electronic light body (also known as your I AM Presence or God Self) into this physical dimension. As this guided meditation progresses, you will notice profound shifts of energy as you begin to activate and anchor your electronic light body into full, conscious, physical reality. **#13**
**A double-cassette of approximately two hours**

# VIDEOTAPES

☆*"AN INTERVIEW WITH AEOLIAH"* ☆ Parts 1 and 2 by New Age reporter **VALLI AMAN** of *VISIONS*. This quality color videotape features the famous Los Angeles New Age reporter, **Valli Aman** during her current television program *VISIONS*. In this full-hour, two part interview, she interviews AEOLIAH on the *Vision* and creation of his music, art, writing, and his personal, spiritual journey. This video features some of Aeoliah's original paintings and excerpts from his music. **#14**

# ORDER FORM

| | Price | Quantity | Amount |
|---|---|---|---|
| Unlaminated Poster | $20.00 | _____ | _____ |
| Laminated Poster | 22.00 | _____ | _____ |
| Unlam., hand-signed Poster | $98.00 | _____ | _____ |

Cassettes Each  (indicate by # and quantity each)

| | $9.98 | _____ | _____ |
|---|---|---|---|
| _____ | $9.98 | _____ | _____ |
| _____ | $9.98 | _____ | _____ |

Compact Discs Each (indicate by # and quantity each)

| | $15.98 | _____ | _____ |
|---|---|---|---|
| _____ | $15.98 | _____ | _____ |
| _____ | $15.98 | _____ | _____ |

*Anchoring Light Body*

| Double Cassette | $14.98 | _____ | _____ |
|---|---|---|---|
| Video: *An Interview w/Aeoliah* | $29.98 | _____ | _____ |
| Additional Copy of Book | $14.95 | _____ | _____ |

Shipping  Costs:     $2.00 for first item, $.75 each additional
                     item, $3.00 for videotape, $3.00 for book

California Residents, add 6% sales tax

Receive a 10% discount for 5 or more items ordered

Enclose payment  by check, money order, or VISA/MasterCard
in an envelope to:    WILLOW MUSIC, INC.

Helios Rising Publications
PO Box 151439
San Rafael, CA.  94915

Phone:  (415) 456-9335     Fax:  (415) 456-5456

VISA/MC #    _____

Exp. date:    _____

Signature    _____

Address      _____

_____

From:

_____

_____

_____

Dear Friends at Willow Music:

☐ I would like to receive a free catalog of your Tapes
and Compact Discs.
☐ I would like to sponsor a seminar in my area.
Please contact me.
☐ I would like to order the following:
(See reverse side)

To:
WILLOW MUSIC INC.
Helios Rising Publications
PO Box 151439
San Rafael, CA. 94915